MAKING PEACE

The United States
and Conflict Resolution

Titles in This Series

Case Studies in International Affairs
Series Editor: Martin Staniland, University of Pittsburgh

The case-study approach to teaching and learning is on the rise in foreign policy and international studies classrooms. Westview Press is pleased to promote this trend by publishing a series of casebooks for a variety of college courses.

Innovative educators are using case studies to:

- Develop critical thinking skills
- Engage students in decisionmaking and role playing
- Transform lecture courses into interactive courses
- Encourage students to apply theoretical concepts using practical experience and knowledge
- Exercise skills in negotiation, management, and leadership

Each book will include theoretical and historical background material, four to eight case studies from all regions of the world, material introducing and connecting the cases, and discussion questions. Teaching notes will be provided to adopting professors and, to encourage the use of several different books and themes within a single class, the casebooks will be short, inexpensive paperbacks of approximately 150 pages.

The individual case studies making up the heart of each volume were developed in conjunction with seven institutions—University of Pittsburgh, Harvard University, Georgetown University, Columbia University, Johns Hopkins University, University of Southern California, and the International Peace Academy—under the auspices of The Pew Charitable Trusts. From over 140 case studies developed by leading scholars, the editors have selected those studies that thematically and substantively offer the best classroom examples for each topic in the series.

MAKING PEACE

The United States and Conflict Resolution

edited by

ALLAN E. GOODMAN and
SANDRA CLEMENS BOGART

Georgetown University

Westview Press

BOULDER ■ SAN FRANCISCO ■ OXFORD

Case Studies in International Affairs

This volume, as compiled, copyright © 1992 by Westview Press, Inc. The following case studies have been edited and are reprinted here with permission: "Making Peace with Germany, 1918: The Pre-Armistice Negotiations" by Robert F. Randle (Pew case study no. 435) copyright © by The Pew Charitable Trusts; "The Suez Crisis, 1956" by Michael G. Fry (Pew case study no. 126) copyright © by The Pew Charitable Trusts; "The Vietnam Negotiations, October–December 1972" by Allan E. Goodman (Pew case study no. 307) copyright © by The Pew Charitable Trusts; "U.S. Mediation in the Falklands/ Malvinas Crisis: Shuttle Diplomacy in the 1980s" by Chaim D. Kaufmann (Pew case study no. 431) copyright © by The Pew Charitable Trusts; and "The Reagan Administration and Lebanon" by Richard Haas and David Kennedy (Pew case study no. 340) copyright © by The Pew Charitable Trusts, the University of Pittsburgh, and the President and Fellows of Harvard College.

Published in 1992 in the United States of America by Westview Press, Inc., 5500 Central Avenue, Boulder, Colorado 80301-2847, and in the United Kingdom by Westview Press, 13 Brunswick Centre, London WC1N 1AF, England

A CIP catalog record for this book is available from the Library of Congress.
ISBN 0-8133-8267-X
ISBN 0-8133-8266-1 (pbk.)

ACF-7692

Printed and bound in the United States of America

The paper used in this publication meets the requirements of the American National Standard for Permanence of Paper for Printed Library Materials Z39.48-1984.

10   9   8   7   6   5   4   3   2   1

CONTENTS

FOREWORD

The Westview series "Case Studies in International Affairs" stems from a major project of the Pew Charitable Trusts entitled "the Pew Diplomatic Initiative." Launched in 1985, this project has sought to improve the teaching and practice of negotiation through adoption of the case-method of teaching, principally in professional schools of international affairs in the United States.

By 1989, authors associated with the seven institutions involved in the Diplomatic Initiative had written over 140 case studies in international negotiation for classroom use.[1] In considering a second phase of the program, the Pew Charitable Trusts determined that its emphasis should shift from writing cases to encouraging their adoption in courses taught through the case-method.

One aspect of this phase has been the establishment of a clearinghouse at the Graduate School of Public and International Affairs, University of Pittsburgh, to distribute and promote the cases. During the first two years of the clearinghouse's operation, it quickly became clear that a sizeable market for the case studies (and a considerable interest in case-method teaching) existed in the larger community of university and college undergraduate instruction. By October 1990, over 15,000 single copies of cases had been sold, and the circle of customers had widened to include instructors in such countries as India, Bulgaria, and the Soviet Union.

It also became clear that, although a classroom use for individual cases would always exist, there was instructional potential in sets of cases selected to illustrate particular issues in negotiation as well as negotiations over particular policy matters. Hence the Westview series, which offers students and instructors the opportunity to examine and discuss specific themes, including themes (such as foreign policymaking) that fall outside of the ambit of international negotiation. Each volume presents a selection of cases, some short, others long, some essentially unchanged, others extensively edited or rewritten. Each volume also contains an introductory chapter, identifying the characteristic features and dilemmas of the kind of negotiation or issue exemplified by the cases. Each volume contains questions for discussion, suggestions for simulation, and further reading.

Case method teaching typically involves two elements. The first (and essential) element is careful reading of a case document by students. The second is one or more classroom sessions in which an instructor, using sustained Socratic questioning, tries to get students to explore the meaning of events that are described, but deliberately not interpreted or explained, in the case document.

Like all teaching, case-method teaching depends on a contract, however implicit. The contract here is framed by two norms: the first is that the material within the case provides a common stock of evidence and an obligatory point of reference. If this norm is broken by the introduction of extraneous or privileged information, the case will cease to serve as a common focus, the assumption of equal information (however artificial and fictitious it may be) will break down, and some students will feel discouraged from participating.

The second norm is one of judgmental equality—that, for purposes of the discussion, the instructor willingly suspends his or her authority for the sake of encouraging students to develop and express their own interpretations of events. Although the instructor may (indeed, should) organize discussions so as to lead students into specific questions, he or she will undermine the exploratory and interactive character of the discussions if students have the impression that they are required to discover "the right answers." This does not mean that instructors have to say (much less to believe) that they have no opinions or that one person's opinion is as good as another's. It simply means that they should be prepared to retreat, temporarily, to the roles of agenda-setter and discussion leader, rather than assuming those of decisionmaker and interpreter.

Although obviously there are some important premises regarding educational philosophy and psychology underpinning belief in case-method teaching, the case for instructors holding back is essentially pragmatic—that discussion is a good educational vehicle and that students will only climb onto it if they are allowed to share in the driving.

Case-method teaching is, then, a tool, supplementing the conventional tools of exposition. Cases can be used to follow up lectures; they can (as this series implies) be used comparatively; they can be used for discussion or for simulation. They can be used with or without accompanying writing assignments. They can be used to illustrate theoretical concepts (such as power) or to require students to enter into the agonies of political choice ("What would you have done if you were President Carter?") But what they invariably do is to enable—and to force—students to take responsibility for their own political and academic education. The faint burning smell of hard thinking hangs in the air after a good case discussion has taken place. Surely anything that produces that smell should be welcome.

Martin Staniland
Series Editor

NOTES

1. The institutions concerned were the School of International Relations, University of Southern California; the School of International and Public Affairs, Columbia University; the Edmund A. Walsh School of Foreign Service, Georgetown University; the John F. Kennedy School of Government, Harvard University; the International Peace Academy (of the United Nations); the Paul H. Nitze School of Advanced International Studies, Johns Hopkins University; and the Graduate School of Public and International Affairs, University of Pittsburgh.

1

INTRODUCTION

All wars end. But not all—or even most—wars end by diplomacy. Prior to the nineteenth century, the majority of wars ended with either a decisive military victory of one country over another or with the surrender of one side, based on the admonitions of military experts and their calculation that victory was militarily or financially inconceivable. At times, if the continuation of conflict was viewed as a threat to the stability or security of other more powerful nations, a settlement was externally imposed, and the war was forced to a reach a conclusion. In relatively few cases, exhaustion or the approximate equality of opposing forces led to stalemate. Frequently, it was the prolongation of this condition that prompted both sides to reevaluate their original war aims and motivated their leaders to seek a rapid settlement in order to end the conflict.

More recently, with the advent of the modern mass army and the introduction of the international balance-of-power concept at the Congress of Vienna, negotiation has become more prevalent as a means of war termination. Between 1800 and 1980, for example, there have been more than sixty interstate wars of which two-thirds ended by negotiation. Civil wars (of which there were twenty-one during this period) and anticolonial wars (fifty-two), however, seem less amenable to negotiated settlement. Roughly one-fifth of these conflicts ended by diplomacy, although negotiation was attempted in nearly every case.[1]

WHY STUDY WAR TERMINATION?

The focus of this book is on the methods of ending military conflicts through negotiated settlements and the special challenges that negotiating for

1

peace poses for diplomatic personnel and, more broadly, for the future welfare of participating nations. The need for expertise and comprehensive knowledge in this area is not likely to diminish in the foreseeable future. Even détentes—or ententes, for that matter—between the most powerful members of an international system do not guarantee that their leaders reject the use of force in the pursuit of future national aims or that a host of lesser powers will settle their disputes peacefully. In addition, although the apparent end of the cold war may reduce the number of conflicts precipitated by East-West tensions, the recent invasions of Panama by the United States and Kuwait by Iraq are stark reminders that warfare remains an operative instrument of foreign policy.

In fact, the potential for renewed regional conflict, over many historically disputed territorial claims, is probably greater in an international system where the superpowers enjoy détente and act with restraint. Under these controlled conditions, in the interest of cooperation, both the Soviet Union and the United States may try to avoid assuming the role of a "world policeman" and refrain from exploiting regional instabilities to the other's disadvantage. Thus, dissident and separatist groups may receive little help from the superpowers, and the United States and the U.S.S.R. may also be unable to exert significant influence over the course of such conflicts. As sources of external assistance are reduced, the struggles will probably take on a more intense character and become dominated by the demands and the outlooks of the extremes. So, in the period ahead, there is likely to be substantial political turmoil and even war in much of the Third World. The prevailing belligerent attitudes in such countries as Iraq, Cuba, North Korea, Libya, and Vietnam present obstacles to peaceful negotiations. These nations appear untouched by trends toward East-West détente and democratization; the leaders of these countries, in fact, seem more rather than less inclined to use force in order to influence regional affairs. In this type of international environment, negotiating for peace will remain one of the most difficult challenges facing nations and their diplomatic representatives.

The subject of war termination is treated in two ways in this book. The introduction presents an overview of the nature of war termination by looking at the issues involved in answering three questions:

1. *What conditions offer the best chance for negotiations during wartime?*
2. *How are war termination negotiations conducted?*
3. *Which strategies promote success in war termination negotiations?*

These questions are then posed with reference to the key turning points in six conflicts in which diplomats attempted to negotiate for peace. Each conflict is presented as an abridged version of the following case studies, which were developed for the Pew Initiative in Diplomatic Training: (1) *Negotiating the End of World War I* is adapted from Robert F. Randle, *Making Peace with Germany, 1918: The Pre-Armistice Negotiations* (Pew case study no. 435). (2) *Concluding the War over Suez* is adapted from Michael G. Fry, *The Suez Crisis, 1956* (Pew case study no. 126). (3) *Ending the Vietnam War* is adapted from Allan E. Goodman, *The Vietnam Negotiations, October-December 1972* (Pew case study no. 307). (4) *Mediation During the War in the Falklands/Malvinas* is adapted from Chaim D. Kaufmann, *U.S. Mediation in the Falklands/Malvinas Crisis: Shuttle Diplomacy in the 1980s* (Pew case study no. 431). (5) *Resolving the Lebanon Crisis* is adapted from Richard Haass and David Kennedy, *The Reagan Administration and Lebanon*, (Pew case study no. 340). (6) *Diplomacy During the Persian Gulf War*, by Allan E. Goodman, is a new case study describing the negotiation process in relation to the recent Persian Gulf war.

These particular conflicts were selected because of their similarity to the types of conflicts that may emerge in the future of international affairs, for the reasons previously mentioned. The original text of each of these cases was considerably longer than could be accommodated in the volumes in this series, so what the authors presented has been abridged, and a common structure has been imposed. The case studies that result, moreover, are sharpened to focus on a few key decision points in the negotiations so that the text promotes the practice of teaching about war termination by asking students to examine the motivations and actions of diplomatic representatives and national leaders and to explore alternative courses of action under the circumstances.

WHAT LEADS TO NEGOTIATIONS DURING WARTIME?

The subject of war termination generally has received very little attention in social science and historical literature, and it is rare in the curricula of most schools and programs of international relations to devote a whole course to the subject. *International Negotiations*, a bibliography published in 1989, contains, for example, a total of twelve references on war termination out of 5,500 citations of English language books, journal articles, doctoral dissertations, government documents, and conference reports.[2] And at the fifteen member institutions of the Association of Professional Schools of International Affairs (APSIA) in the United States, only a handful of courses in history and international relations devote substantial time to the study of how wars can be ended (versus how they start). Devoting such scant teaching resources to the subject of war termination—especially the practicalities involved in the actual process—is probably justified on the premise that it is unlikely that many of the future diplomats being educated today will find themselves actually involved in negotiations to end a war. All students will find themselves negotiating situations of conflict—and most will want to seek peaceful resolution. In a broad sense, the cases serve as a laboratory for the practical application of knowledge by allowing students to correlate theoretical principles to specific cases. Each case also contributes to students' understanding of historical detail and negotiating mechanics by illustrating the chronology and perspectives of the period and examining the strategies and techniques of the negotiating process. The subject is important in the procedural training of diplomats as well, because most who have been involved in war termination efforts came to the assignment largely by surprise. There is really no way of predicting who, among today's students, might eventually need to master and implement the methods of promoting peace.

Furthermore, the rationale for initiating negotiations during wartime is still not very clear. The few systematic studies that have been conducted to study potential relationships between such quantitative variables as casualty levels, the size of and asymmetries between the opposing forces, and the length of a war and the likelihood of a negotiated settlement of the conflict, moreover, "have not been particularly conclusive."[3] This, of course, does not mean that such indicators of military power and effectiveness are irrelevant, only that, in isolation, they do not appear to provide the stimulus for the leaders of belligerent states or guerrilla and separatist forces to decide to risk negotiating while fighting. In cases where such negotiation occurs, the parties to the conflict may be disingenuous about working toward a legitimate settlement and choose to manipulate the process, using it to buy time and weaken the will of their opponents.[4]

Therefore, perhaps the best starting point to understanding why wars end through solutions arranged by diplomats is to initially consider the act of war itself in political terms. Thus, the following observation by Carl von Clausewitz is particularly useful for framing an answer to the question of what conditions offer the best chance for negotiations during wartime:

> Since war is not an act of senseless passion but is controlled by its political object, the value of this object must determine the sacrifices made for it in magnitude and also in duration. Once the expenditure of effort exceeds the value of the political object, the object must be renounced and peace must follow.[5]

Although some wars occur inadvertently, most of them are the result of a conscious decision by the leadership of a state or other organization to seek political objectives (e.g., power, autonomy) by military means. In making this decision, the leaders have in mind not only what they want to achieve but also an estimate of how long it is likely to take to secure this objective and at what cost. Clausewitz is pointing out to negotiators the importance of looking for the turning points—and the pressures and developments on the battlefield that one might reasonably predict would provoke them—that raise doubts, not regarding the original aim of the war, but of the initial estimates of its cost and duration. If these doubts can be ascertained by at least one side, it is likely that the conflict could be settled by bargaining over the terms for a cease-fire and some form of a political settlement.

Is the element of doubt a mutual requirement? For negotiations to succeed in reaching a settlement—which, by definition, allows each side to gain some but not all of its objectives—the answer to this question is probably yes. For if one side of a military conflict remains convinced that they have the time and resources to achieve their original goals—or that they have no real alternatives to pursuing victory that would be politically acceptable and allow them to remain in power—they may enter negotiations with a slate of concealed motives, such as testing the determination of the other side to continue to fight or allowing time to regroup their forces and prepare for a new offensive.

Accordingly, in each of the cases featured in this volume, the reader will want to look for those pressures and developments that affected the leaders' assessments of the value of the war objectives—i.e., the expected benefits of continuing the war when weighed against its mounting costs—as well as the degree to which these perceptions are shared by the parties to the conflict. The key variables to look for are the following:

1. stalemates, i.e., conditions under which neither side seems able to prevail by following the strategy and tactics with which they began the war;
2. resource constraints, which occur as a result of sudden or unforeseen changes in the manner in which both sides planned to finance the war, or which serve to rule out a change in strategy and tactics;
3. external political and economic pressure from allies and neighbors to end the conflict, because its continuation threatens their security; and
4. internal political pressures and changes, which prompt leaders to rethink the wisdom of continued fighting, or to doubt their ability to mobilize the public support necessary to maintain the level of sacrifice required to fight rather than negotiate.

The student should aim at developing both an understanding of the motives for initiating a war and the evolution and transformation of such motives, over the course of the conflict, in ways that allow the diplomats—and require the leaders—to propose that negotiating is preferable to battle.

THE PROCESS AND DYNAMICS OF WAR TERMINATION NEGOTIATIONS

There is no standard process for negotiating an end to warfare. In some cases, armistice talks are proposed and occur instantaneously (e.g., World War I); in other situations, talks about talks may continue for years before actual bargaining about the specific terms of a settlement begins (e.g., Vietnam, 1962-1971). In still other cases, negotiations may begin almost simultaneously with the fighting (e.g., Suez) but later become deadlocked as each side prepares to escalate the conflict (Falklands/Malvinas). Despite such variation, it is still helpful to identify specific phases in the negotiation process—phases that may vary considerably in length. In each phase, moreover, certain key decisions have to be reached. Consequently, each of the case studies is organized to stimulate analysis and discussion of the following.

The Decision to Negotiate. In this phase of negotiation the parties to a conflict explore the possibility of settling their differences by negotiating.[6] Such "prenegotiation" activities can range from the activities of civilian decisionmakers and opinion leaders who begin to question the assumptions of the necessity of the war or the likelihood of its being won to the initial stirring of public discontent with the sacrifices required to continue the fighting. These activities may also include the development and receipt of new sources of information regarding the strength, motives, and current objectives of the adversary.

Getting the Belligerents to the Table. This phase of the war termination process involves the attempts by diplomats and leaders to set a time, place, and agenda for an actual meeting. Negotiations to end a war can take place in many different ways and in many diverse locations. For instance, the setting may be as rugged as a tent or other temporary structure erected near the front lines of the fighting or as elegant as a grand palace in a neutral country, which has lent its good offices to facilitate reaching a settlement. Diplomatic representatives may remain stationary for the duration of a conference or they may continuously travel back and forth between the capitals of the warring parties. Mediators may choose to remain on neutral ground or shuttle between the countries of the combatants with new proposals and ideas regarding the arrangement of a settlement.

The Decisions Required to Break Deadlocks in Bargaining. Negotiations to end a war rarely proceed smoothly. Ironically, it often appears that the closer bargainers move toward reaching a settlement, the more difficult it becomes to secure the final deal. Negotiations may be disturbed if fighting resumes or if the credibility of the bargaining representatives is undermined by government leaders. Adversaries also may want to use the negotiation process to test their opponent's attitudes and the degree of flexibility and desperation apparent in their attempt to reach a settlement. In fact, they may deliberately introduce deadlocks in order to gauge their opponent's reaction. At times the diplomatic representatives may report on the nature of the impending agreement only to learn that top policymakers have changed their attitudes regarding the desirability of an agreement or that important new domestic actors have entered the picture and are unhappy with the terms. Domestic pressures can be exerted by such diverse groups as economic and trade interests, defense industry lobbyists, religious groups, social or environmental activists, peace activists, labor unions, U.N. organizations, members of Congress, Pentagon officials, the National Security Council (NSC), the Central Intelligence Agency (CIA), cabinet members, or by such policy concerns as budgetary restrictions or impending elections. Whatever the cause, in most negotiations there comes a time when neither side seems willing or able to take another step in the direction of settlement. This deadlock, which may be accompanied by a stalemate on the battlefield as well, must be broken if the war is to be ended by diplomacy.

WHICH STRATEGIES PROMOTE SUCCESS?

Any attempt at negotiating the end to a military conflict—as is the case in most things that are bargained over—requires the definition of concrete goals and the determination of the best means of achieving them. Regardless of how suddenly the opportunity for negotiation occurs, the diplomatic representatives, policymakers, and other participants need to approach the bargaining with a well-conceived plan of action. This plan relates ends to means, and in this sense it is the operational definition of strategy.

Ideally, strategy should be formulated well in advance of sitting down to bargain and should focus on the comprehensive "big picture." However, many negotiators, especially those dealing with crises or other situations where the stakes and tensions are high, find that they must react quickly and have little time for such planning. Consequently, many handbooks on negotiation tend to blur the distinction between strategy and tactics and concentrate on the role that the clever use of tactics—or artful resistance to them—can play in achieving a successful outcome.[7]

Strategic planning involves the analysis of why certain goals are being pursued and the extent to which they may be—and are likely to be—altered as a result of the bargaining process. In the case of war termination negotiations, it is useful to consider three alternative "guiding principles," which explain the motives and tactics of the adversaries when they arrive at the bargaining table.

Accommodation. The desire to reach an agreement by recognizing the legitimacy of the other side's position and objectives and then progressively and creatively trying to find ways to partially satisfy these objectives, in order to stop the fighting and/or reduce the chances that it will resume.

Transformation. The use of diplomacy to gain what force appears increasingly unlikely to achieve. In this situation, the adversaries are attempting to obtain the best deal possible but are also desperate to reach an agreement, regardless of the terms, because they are unwilling or unable to continue fighting much longer.

Innovation. With this approach, the adversaries plan to use whatever means necessary to get an agreement, but they are also prepared to walk away from the bargaining table if their opponent cannot be persuaded to accept the proposed terms.

Currently, there are no conclusive findings in social science literature that enable any of us to determine which of these basic strategies (and the range of tactics associated with them) is preferable for ending a war: All have records of success and failure. Others will want to add to this list or suggest better descriptive labels. Each strategy is most likely to be effective, however, if the aforementioned conditions appear to be fulfilled. That is, there must be some considerable degree of mutuality involved in the bargaining process. For example, in order for accommodation to serve as an effective strategy, the commitment to legitimacy and creativity must be present on both sides. Similarly, if transformation is expected to achieve results, the military situation and the domestic, economic, and political considerations must all point in the direction of devising a deal that is essential to both sides. Correspondingly, if the strategy of innovation is to function, both sides must have the inclination to enter into negotiations as well as the will to abandon them and resume the fighting if a settlement cannot be arranged.

KEY DECISION POINTS

In every negotiation there are turning points, at which the diplomats and the leaders they represent make vital decisions regarding their future actions. These decisions range from such considerations as how to respond to an offer, especially if it is one that was unanticipated, to whether or not to continue the negotiations when progress appears slow or the other side behaves as if they were negotiating for side effects. In every case, the decisions are influenced by domestic events and constraints as well as by international considerations.

The analysis of such key decision points is really the focus of each of the case studies presented here. The reader is invited to examine why a particular course of action was taken and also to evaluate whether practical alternatives were available. Particularly in today's complex international system, when the process of negotiating for peace holds much significance for the future, the lessons and wisdom of the past should not be ignored.

NOTES

1. See the statistics compiled by Paul R. Pillar, *Negotiating Peace: War Termination as a Bargaining Process* (Princeton: Princeton University Press, 1983), pp. 9-25. Using several older studies and his own research, Pillar classified every war since 1800 that involved at least 1,000 battle deaths if the conflict lasted less than a year or 1,000 battle deaths annually.

2. Amos Lakos, *International Negotiations: A Bibliography* (Boulder, CO: Westview Press, 1989). The best books addressing this subject that I have found and used are Pillar, *Negotiating for Peace*; Stephen J. Cimbala and Keith A. Dunn, eds., *Conflict Termination and Military Strategy: Coercion, Persuasion, and War* (Boulder, CO: Westview Press, 1987); Fred C. Ikle, *Every War Must End* (New York: Columbia University Press, 1971); Paul Kecskemeti, *Strategic Surrender* (Stanford, CA: Stanford University Press, 1958); and Robert F. Randle, *The Origins of Peace* (New York: Free Press, 1973).

3. Pillar, *Negotiating Peace*, p. 6. This judgment is also confirmed by the more recent findings about the relationship between the size and superiority of land and naval forces and air power growing out of a conference at the U.S. Naval War College. See Robert B. Killebrew, "The Role of Ground Forces in Conflict Termination," in Cimbala and Dunn, *Conflict Termination and Military Strategy*, pp. 123-142; Thomas Fabyanic, "Air Power and Conflict Termination," *Ibid.*, pp. 143-160; and Linton F. Brooks, "Conflict Termination Through Maritime Leverage," *Ibid.*, pp. 161-172. Killebrew and Brooks were military officers (navy and army, respectively) when they wrote these articles. Dr. Fabyanic wrote as the vice president of a consulting firm; he is a retired air force officer.

4. For more detail on this aspect of diplomacy, see the discussion of negotiating for "side effects" in Fred C. Ikle, *How Nations Negotiate* (New York: Praeger, 1964), pp. 42-58.

5. Carl von Clausewitz, *On War*, edited and translated by Michael Howard and Peter Paret (Princeton: Princeton University Press, 1976), p. 92.

6. Harold H. Saunders, "The Pre-Negotiation Phase," in Diane B. Bendahmane and John W. McDonald, Jr., eds., *International Negotiation: Art*

and Science (Washington, DC: U.S. Department of State, Foreign Service Institute, 1984), pp. 47-56.

7. See, for example, the books prepared as a result of courses on negotiations for government and business managers by Roger Fisher and William Ury, *Getting to Yes: Negotiating Agreement Without Giving In* (Boston: Houghton Mifflin, 1981); Chester Karass, *The Negotiating Game* (New York: Thomas Y. Crowell Publishers, 1970); Gerard Nierenberg, *Fundamentals of Negotiating* (New York: Hawthorne Books, 1973); and Howard Raiffa, *The Art and Science of Negotiation* (Cambridge, MA: Harvard University Press, 1982). In such handbooks, the authors indicate that they have found that most negotiators tend to think in tactical rather than strategic terms even if they initially hoped to do the opposite. On the difficulties involved in teaching strategy to negotiators, and for some suggestions about how it can be done, see Allan E. Goodman, "Teaching Strategy in Negotiation," *Negotiation Journal*, vol. 6 (April 1990), pp. 185-188.

2

NEGOTIATING THE END OF WORLD WAR I, 1918

After the United States declared war on Germany in April 1917, President Woodrow Wilson knew that the task of making peace would be difficult. But he also knew that it would offer the United States an unparalleled opportunity to introduce a new world order based on a scheme of collective security and on the principles of justice and democratic ideals that the president and a majority of Americans believed had worked so successfully in the United States. The focus of this case is on the series of critical decisions that had to be made when the opportunity for ending the war materialized.

REACHING THE DECISION TO NEGOTIATE

The chance for peace arose in the early fall of 1918 with an unexpected suddenness. In late 1917, Wilson had attempted to convince the Entente powers to formulate and publicize more moderate war aims than they had theretofore proclaimed—war aims that could serve as the basis for a just peace. In this initiative, he appeared at first to have failed. Wilson therefore decided to move ahead with a unilateral declaration of enormous propaganda value that would raise the morale of the Allies, preemptively commit them to a liberal peace, and weaken the Central Powers by attracting the left-of-center parties in Germany and Austria-Hungary. He was also prompted to take this

---

This chapter is an edited version of the case study by Robert F. Randle, Making Peace with Germany, 1918: The Pre-Armistice Negotiations, *Pew case study no. 435.*

step because the Bolsheviks, who had won control of the cities of Petrograd and Moscow in the November Revolution, had published the secret treaties between the czar and the Allies. The president and his advisers were concerned about the impact the revelations of secret international bargaining in the old style (between the Russian autocracy, France, and Great Britain) might have on public opinion. But Wilson also believed that his principles might be attractive to the Bolsheviks and might persuade them to remain in the fight against Germany. Wilson consequently asked his adviser, Colonel Edward M. House, to form a panel of experts to produce a peace plan. This group, which came to be known as The Inquiry, furnished the president with studies that were to supplement and develop his own ideas for peace.

Before a Joint Session of Congress on 8 January 1918, the president, in a historic address, listed fourteen points that he thought essential for the restoration of peace and the creation of a new world order. The Fourteen Points were a succinct statement of the specific principles that had up to that time been U.S. war aims, along with several more general principles that would guarantee a world order in the postwar era so stable that the outbreak of another war would be unlikely, if not impossible. In the category of specific principles, the president called for the evacuation of Germany from Belgium and the complete restoration of Belgian sovereignty (Point 7); the freeing and restoration of French territory and retrocession of the Alsace-Lorraine to France (Point 8); readjustment of the frontiers of Italy "along clearly recognizable lines of nationality" (Point 9); the creation of a Polish state in territories "inhabited by indisputably Polish populations," with access to the sea, guaranteed by international covenant (Point 13); and evacuation of all Russian territory and a settlement for Russia that would "assure her of a sincere welcome into the society of free nations under institutions of her own choosing" (Point 6). Romania, Serbia, and Montenegro were to be evacuated. Serbia would be given access to the sea, and the Balkan states would be given international guarantees of political and economic independence (Point 11). With respect to Austria-Hungary and the Ottoman Empire, in Point 10, Wilson in effect called for the application of the principle of national self-determination: "The peoples of Austria-Hungary, whose place among the nations we wish to see safeguarded and assured, should be accorded the freest opportunity of autonomous development." And while the Turkish portions of the Ottoman Empire should be assured sovereignty, similarly, its non-Turkish nationalities were to be assured security of life and autonomous development (Point 12).

Perhaps the most famous of the *general* principles for establishing a permanent peace was Point 14, which called for the creation, by specific covenants, of an association of nations that would provide mutual guarantees of political independence and territorial integrity. Wilson also called for freedom of navigation on the high seas, the removal of economic barriers to world trade, and the reduction of armaments (Points 2-4). He declared that diplomacy should always proceed frankly and in public view and that covenants of peace should be "open" and openly arrived at (Point 1). Finally, with respect to the settlement of colonial claims, he claimed that the interests of the populations concerned should have equal weight with the claims of the European states that governed them (Point 5).[1]

In subsequent addresses, the president further developed his peace plans. On the recommendation of his advisers, he even more directly appealed to the German Left in a speech before a Joint Session of Congress on 11 February 1918. There should be no annexations, he declared, no reparations.

> Peoples are not to be handed about from one sovereignty to another by an international conference or an understanding between rivals and antagonists. National aspirations must be respected; peoples may now be dominated and governed only by their own consent. 'Self-determination' is not a mere phrase. It is an imperative principle of action, which statesmen henceforth ignore at their peril.[2]

In two of the Four Principles (as they came to be called), he again stressed the necessity for according recognition to national aspirations. Peoples, he declared, should not be "bartered about as . . . if they were mere chattels and pawns in a game, even the great game, now forever discredited, of the balance of power." He also declared that each part of a peace settlement must be based upon the essential justice of the particular case and upon adjustments that would assure a permanent peace.

> So far as we can judge, these principles that we regard as fundamental are already everywhere accepted as imperative except among the spokesmen of the military and annexationist party in Germany . . . . The tragical circumstance is that this one party in Germany is apparently willing and able to send millions of men to their death to prevent what all the world now sees to be just.[3]

In the United States, the president's program was greeted with acclaim, as it was among what Arno Mayer calls the parties of "movement" in Britain and France. The French were particularly gratified that Wilson had so unequivocally declared that Alsace-Lorraine must be retroceded to France (without, incidentally, consulting the "interests of the populations"). It is noteworthy that British Prime Minister David Lloyd George had made a speech in many respects similar to Wilson's three days earlier in the House of Commons. It was also noteworthy that he did not mention open diplomacy, the lowering of tariff barriers, or freedom of the seas. Given the real and symbolic importance of the Royal Navy for the British, their cool reaction to Wilson's call for "absolute freedom of navigation of the seas, outside territorial waters, alike in peace and war" (Point 2) was understandable.

The Fourteen Points also evoked a favorable response from German businessmen, journalists, and those who favored a compromise peace. In late February, a coordinating committee for the Reichstag's majority parties on the Left agreed to accept the Fourteen Points as a basis for peace, provided that all territory of the German Reich was retained. For those in control of German war policy, however, Wilson's program appeared to have no influence. A great German offensive on the western front was mounted in March; in the same month, the German government imposed the Treaty of Brest-Litovsk upon Russia, a settlement that was the very antithesis of the peace Wilson sought.

As a result of the Treaty of Brest-Litovsk, Germany gained a tremendous tactical advantage. Russia was out of the war, thus eliminating the German problem of a two-front battle. In addition, German control over large areas of European Russia was officially sanctioned. At this time, Russia became entangled in a state of continuous civil war, as resistance to the Bolsheviks became increasingly militant and the battle in Russia turned inward. Perceiving a unique opportunity to exploit the chaotic situation to the disadvantage of both the Germans and the Bolsheviks, the Allies sanctioned a joint intervention in Russia. Although it was primarily intended to prevent Russian supplies from falling into German hands, this mission was also designed to provide some degree of Allied support for anti-Bolshevik forces.

In a speech in April, the president declared that, in view of the desperate struggle then being fought in France, it was essential for the United States to fight side by side with the Allies until victory was won. Even in these circumstances, with the president sounding very much like a war leader, he continued to assert that the German people would be treated fairly after their defeat.

The German offensive of late March 1918 made impressive progress at first. The war of stalemate and attrition appeared to have given way once again to a war of movement. The Germans reached the Marne, slowed their advance for resupply, and then attacked again across the Marne in mid-July. Given advance warning of this offensive, however, Marshal Ferdinand Foch, commander in chief of the Allied armies in France, prepared a strategy to meet it and to strike back when the time was opportune. He was able to counterattack on 18 July with French and U.S. troops, along a 45-kilometer front between Soissons and Rheims. The Germans were forced back across the Marne. With this limited setback in the Champagne region, they had lost the initiative; and indeed, they had permanently lost it on the entire western front, although only somewhat later did the German High Command and the Allies themselves realize that this was a turning point of the war. They certainly could not escape this realization when Anglo-French armies struck them by surprise east of Amiens on 8 August. The Germans were forced into a four-day retreat back to the Somme. The German government and the High Command now faced a serious situation. Throughout late spring and summer, they had been able to ignore the factiousness of the parties of the Left in the Reichstag that were calling for a negotiated peace, a peace of compromise without forcible annexations, and they had dismissed Austrian pressures for peace as defeatism. They had felt they could win the war with a resolute army and people, in spite of the shortages of essential foods, cloth, coal and many metals, and the influenza epidemic. But after the retreat to the Somme, terrible doubts about the effectiveness of their army and the war's outcome arose within the High Command and even among the political leaders of the Center and the Right who had access to the real news coming from the front. The German army was defeated at Arras in early September, at Saint-Mihiel in the middle of the month, and at Saint-Quentin and in the Meuse-Argonne in late September. Bulgaria was about to surrender to the invading Entente armies, and Damascus was under attack and surrendered to the British in late September. The Austrian note of 14 September, appealing to all the belligerents to send delegates to a neutral country to discuss the terms of peace, had come as a shock to the Germans: It appeared that their ally had concluded that continuation of the war would mean defeat and possible invasion of the homeland, and the note implied a willingness to conclude a separate peace.

The Austrian peace note had received a mixed reception in Britain and rejection by the French premier, Georges Clemenceau. Wilson's reply to the note was the following:

> The government of the United States feels that there is only one reply which it can make to the suggestion of the Imperial AustroHungarian Government. It has repeatedly and with entire candor stated the terms upon which the United States would consider peace and can and will entertain no proposal for a conference upon a matter concerning which it has made its position and purpose so plain.[4]

What could Austria, or the other Central Powers for that matter, expect if they were to request an armistice from their positions of increasing weakness in the fall of 1918? The publics of the Entente powers were not only weary of the war, but they were also deeply embittered by the costs and duration of the war effort that they believed had been thrust upon them by the aggression of the German and Austrian militarists in 1914 and by the barbarity (as they saw it) of the German, Austrian, and Turkish armed forces.

In the United States, active belligerency had inevitably created an atmosphere of hatred for the enemy. In the summer of 1918, the Republicans, in anticipation of the upcoming congressional elections in the fall, declared that only a Republican-controlled Congress could win a complete victory and promote a sound domestic transition to peace. In August, Senator Henry Cabot Lodge, Republican of Massachusetts, had taken a hard-line position and insisted that the war must end in the unconditional surrender of Germany. There must be a peace dictated inside German territory, he declared. Any prospective armistice or peace treaty would almost certainly be a dominant election issue.

On 27 September, President Wilson made another unusually important speech, opening the Fourth Liberty Loan campaign in New York City. He intended it to influence not only his U.S. audience but the Allied and German peoples as well. The president had been repeatedly urged to reassert that liberal vision of the peace he so eloquently described in the early months of 1918. Most of Wilson's advisers, including Colonel House, William C. Bullitt (a State Department adviser) and journalist Walter Lippmann, feared that the president had recently been too readily giving the impression of inflexibility toward Germany. Pursuit of too hard a line, they feared, might not only alienate European liberals, but perhaps even strengthen the German militarists. They argued that Wilson ought to try to induce the Entente powers to accept the Fourteen Points while they were still very much dependent upon U.S. support. Wilson agreed with these advisers, especially because he did not want the U.S. people to equate his commitment to win the war in cooperation with the Allies to U.S. support for any Allied imperialist aims. He was also sensitive to the need to challenge the Republican leaders' demand for a punitive peace in the upcoming congressional elections and to avoid a prolonged war by removing the basis of the German autocrats' argument against an armistice.

In the New York address, Wilson declared that there could be no special or selfish political alliances or economic combinations within a League of Nations. No special interests of any one nation or group of nations could be the basis of a settlement unless it was consistent with the interests of all. He also declared, "The impartial justice meted out must involve no discrimination between those to whom we wish to be just and those to whom we do not wish to be just. It must be a justice that plays no favorites, and knows no standards but the equal rights of the several peoples concerned."[5]

In late September, the Germans sustained additional reverses on the battlefields of France. Bulgaria's resistance collapsed and the Bulgarian government asked for armistice terms. And in Berlin and at Spa, the political crisis deepened. In this atmosphere, Chancellor George von Hertling resigned on 29 September. A new government, under Prince Max of Baden, was formed on 3 October and was authorized to seek an armistice. It did so in a note dispatched on the 4th. On the 7th, the Swiss minister formally presented the German note in Washington. On the same day, the U.S. government also received a request for an armistice from Austria-Hungary.

The German note to Wilson read:

The German Government requests the President of the United States to take steps for the restoration of peace, to notify all belligerents of this request, and to invite them to delegate plenipotentiaries for the purpose of taking up negotiations. The German Government accepts, as a basis for the peace negotiations, the program laid down by the President . . . in his message to Congress of January 8, 1918, and his subsequent pronouncements, particularly in his address of September 27, 1918.

In order to avoid further bloodshed the German Government requests the President to bring about the immediate conclusion of an armistice on land, on water, and in the air.

[signed] Max, Prince of Baden
Imperial Chancellor[6]

DISCUSSION QUESTIONS

1. *How does President Wilson see the diplomatic and military situation at this point?*
2. *What are the key assumptions Wilson is making about his adversaries and allies?*
3. *How should President Wilson respond to the note from the German Chancellor?*
4. *What are the alternative policies he might follow at this point?*

GETTING TO THE TABLE

Wilson decided that the German note needed clarification. He rejected a suggestion that he consult the Allies, because he perceived that matters were at too preliminary a stage and consultation would cause delay. The president was aware that the British, French, and, to a lesser extent, the Italians all knew the contents of the German note and were concerned about his failure to immediately communicate with them. Indeed, the Allies' prime ministers met in Paris on 5 October. Without inviting General Tasker H. Bliss, the U.S. representative to the Supreme War Council, to participate, they adopted a set of guidelines for an armistice with Germany. On the 8th, the War Council, consisting of the military and naval representatives of the Allies, produced a somewhat more detailed set of guidelines, which Bliss was then asked to sign. In view of the fact that he had no instructions from Washington, he declined to do so.

While a U.S. reply was being drafted, the Senate debated the armistice question. The president was surprised by the "war-mad" sentiment among Senate Republicans and, indeed, in the country generally, a sentiment that was opposed to accepting anything but an unconditional surrender from the Germans. He also disclosed to Colonel House that he was upset by the Supreme War Council's action in independently drafting armistice guidelines, not only because they failed to consult him but also because he believed it was a mistake to go into details with the Germans at the time.

Wilson received advice from many quarters. He was certainly aware of U.S. public opinion and the possible consequences of his mishandling of the reply to the German note. He knew, on the one hand, of the widespread longing, even the need, for peace; he knew, on the other, that Germany must not be permitted to use an armistice or prearmistice negotiations to rebuild its strength. The unanimous disapproval of his advisers might have prevented him from making a reply or offering concessions. However, his advisers encouraged him to proceed with the course he announced to them because by outright rejection of the German bid the president would lose both an opportunity for ending a tragic war and the chance to fulfill his vision of a just peace.

On 8 October, the president replied to the German note. The press was given a copy of the reply with the statement that it was not really a "reply but an inquiry." His note posed two questions: whether the Chancellor meant "that the Imperial German Government accepts the terms laid down by the President in his address . . . on the 8th of January last and in subsequent addresses and that its object in entering into discussions would be only to agree upon the practical details of application"; and second, whether "the Imperial Chancellor is speaking merely for the constituted authorities of the Empire who have so far conducted the war." He also demanded the immediate withdrawal of Central Powers forces from invaded territory, prior to the initiation of any negotiations to end the conflict.[7]

The Allied prime ministers, when informed of the nature of Wilson's "inquiry," were upset that he had not yet consulted them. They sent him two notes on 10 October. The first agreed with him that the evacuation of territory was a preliminary condition of all discussion with the Germans. But it was not a sufficient condition, and others must be imposed that would prevent the enemy from profiting by a cessation of hostilities. Military experts must be consulted, they asserted. The second note appealed to Wilson to send an U.S. representative to Paris with full powers because, in the circumstances, decisions at short notice might soon have to be taken.

Much of the press in France and Italy did approve of the president's note, as did the French Socialist party and the Commission on Foreign Affairs of the French Chamber of Deputies. The British press was somewhat less laudatory but for the most part did not disapprove. Although British policymakers resented the fact that the Germans had made the appeal for an armistice to Wilson, and not to them, their desire for an early peace and recognition of the dangers of a confrontation with the president over the issues at this time tempered their anger. But the British leaders' frustration and indignation continued unabated. The political realities of the domestic situation had to be faced. Labor unrest, including a police strike, and discontent in the Royal Navy suggested that a prolongation of the war was undesirable and perhaps even dangerous to political stability.

The U.S. Senate also continued to debate the question of an armistice and its terms. Leading Republicans remained openly, and indeed bitterly, critical of Wilson's whole approach.

On 12 October, a passenger-carrying mail steamer, the *Leinster*, was sunk by a German submarine in the Irish Sea, with the loss of 450 lives. The outrage of public opinion among the Allies and the bitter criticism of Germany hardly conduced to a cool and reasoned approach to the demarche for peace that the Germans had made. In his memoirs, Prince Max of Baden, having just approved the draft of a reply to President Wilson, later wrote, "Not since the *Lusitania* had sorrow and anger been so great in England and America. We had indeed recalled the submarines from the American coast, but unfortunately had neglected to anticipate such a catastrophe, which could have been taken in reckoning as things were."[8] The second German note of 12 October declared that Germany "accepted" Wilson's terms of 8 January (i.e., the Fourteen Points) and the principles he had subsequently enunciated: "Consequently its object in entering into discussions would be only to agree upon practical details of the application of these terms." The note went on to observe: "The German Government believes that the Governments of the powers associated with the United States also accept the position taken by President Wilson in his addresses."[9] Certainly this was not a foregone conclusion at this time, and one of Wilson's important objectives was to obtain Allied acceptance of his peace principles. The German government's assertion was an indication of the importance it placed upon all the parties accepting Wilsonian principles as a basis for the negotiations for an armistice and a peace settlement. The note went on to say that Germany stood ready to comply with the "propositions of the President in regard to evacuation," as did Austria-Hungary. The chancellor suggested that a mixed commission be formed for making arrangements for such an evacuation. With respect to the authority of the chancellor and his government, the note concluded: "The present German Government . . . has been formed by conferences and in agreement with the great majority of the Reichstag. The Chancellor, supported in all of his actions by the will of the majority, speaks in the name of the German Government and of the German people."[10]

The State Department felt that the German reply was satisfactory and Secretary of State Robert Lansing urged moderation. But Senate Republicans remained vehemently critical. Nor did the British think the reply adequate. They were especially perturbed because they believed the Germans had no intention of giving up the Alsace-Lorraine (or areas with Polish inhabitants) and that an armistice was simply a cover for the German military to increase their strength and resume the fighting when it was opportune. Moreover, the British strongly objected to several of the Fourteen Points; the Allies, they felt, must not be deprived of the necessary freedom of action in negotiating the settlement at a peace conference by general principles such as these. They felt that Wilson's approach was high-handed, amateurish, and dangerous. But they still recognized that a breach with Washington must be avoided.

The president decided to send Colonel House to Europe immediately. (He was to arrive in France on 25 October.) He also told the press that the United States would continue to send 250,000 men a month to France and there would be "no relaxation of any kind."[11]

The U.S. reply to the second German note, dispatched on 14 October, reached the Germans on the 16th. This note too was immediately released to the press. It was at once accusatory and specific with respect to conditions it required Germany to meet. The process of evacuation and the conditions of an armistice, it declared, must be left to the judgment of the Allies and the United States and must provide guarantees for the maintenance of their present military superiority. The United States would not consent to consider an armistice "so long as the armed forces of Germany continue their illegal and inhumane practices which they persist in . . .; [for example] the sinking of passenger ships, and . . . the very boats in which their passengers and crews seek to make their way to safety . . .; and in their present enforced withdrawal from Flanders and France the German armies are pursuing a course of wanton destruction." As a condition precedent to peace, a definite and satisfactory political guarantee would have to be provided:

It is necessary . . . that the President should . . . call the attention of the Government of Germany to the language and plain intent of one of the terms of peace which the German Government has now accepted. It is contained in the address of the President delivered at Mount Vernon on the Fourth of July last. It is as follows: "The destruction of every arbitrary power anywhere that can separately, secretly, and of its single choice disturb the peace of the world; or, if it cannot be presently destroyed, at least its reduction to virtual impotency." The power which has hitherto controlled the German nation is of the sort here described. It is within the choice of the German nation to alter it.[12]

The tenor of this note, certainly harsher (at least from the German point of view) than might have been expected from President Wilson, could be accounted for by the pressure he was feeling from the many critical voices in the United States and by the state of public opinion after the sinking of the *Leinster*. He was genuinely distressed about the country's intolerant hatred of the Germans and the fact that the desire for vengeance might force the United States to continue the fight against Germany longer than necessary to achieve its objectives. The German scholar Klaus Schwabe adduced other reasons. He wrote that the president understood

> that the Allies would accept neither armistice nor peace terms which did not satisfy their interests, and . . . that they would not hesitate to act independently if they felt it necessary to do so. If Wilson did not want to risk splitting the united front of the Associated Powers and thus destroying the link which he had created between the granting of an armistice and the German acceptance of the Fourteen Points, he could not afford to be wrong in procedural matters. Furthermore, he had to accept publicly the basic principles of the armistice which the Allies wanted, and he had to dispel the false impression which the Allies had that he was ready to negotiate, on an equal footing, with the present German government.[13]

On 19 October, Wilson finally replied to the Austrian request for an armistice, which had been delivered to him two weeks before. The same factors that were at work in shaping the tone and content of the president's second note to the Germans were operative in inducing him to write a frank and firm response to Vienna. But other factors were also at work: the Hapsburg Empire was even then disintegrating, and several of its formerly subject nationalities had declared independence. In view of this, the president decided he must modify Point 10 of the Fourteen Points, which had called for the freest opportunity of autonomous development of the peoples of Austria-Hungary. Because the United States had recognized the state of belligerency between the Czecho-Slovak National Council and the Central Powers and the justice of the national aspirations of the Czecho-Slovaks and the Jugo-Slavs, "[the] President is, therefore, no longer at liberty to accept the "mere" autonomy of these peoples as a basis for peace, but is obliged to insist that they, and not he, shall be the judges of what action on the part of the Austro-Hungarian government will satisfy their aspirations and their conception of their rights and destiny as members of the family of nations."[14]

Not only did this note formally associate the United States government with a policy supporting the dissolution of the Hapsburg Empire, but from Wilson's position it could be inferred that he might similarly modify other of his publicly proclaimed peace terms with prejudice to the Central Powers.

This possibility deeply disturbed the German government. At the same time that Wilson sent this note to Vienna, he assured the French ambassador that he would respect France's policy that no encouragement be given to the merger of Austria and Germany.

The Republican senators who had previously been highly critical of Wilson generally did approve his note of the 14th because it appeared that the president had taken a tougher line with the enemy. With the forthcoming congressional elections of 5 November very much in mind, however, they found much to criticize. The Republican Congressional Committee called the idea of absolutely free trade (the third of the Fourteen Points) an invitation to disaster and urged the election of a Republican Congress to prevent that from happening. With much prescience, the Democrats wondered if a Senate under the leadership of Senator Lodge would ratify any peace treaties embodying Wilson's program. The president still had his supporters, of course, but they appeared to be on the defensive. In spite of the vocal opposition and the widespread hatred of the Germans, Wilson remained intent upon realizing his conception of a just peace. This was revealed by the interview he gave Sir William Wiseman of the British Secret Service in the United States on 16 October. Wiseman was a close friend of Colonel House and would later work closely with him in Paris. To Wiseman, Wilson revealed that he intended to stick by his Fourteen Points. National self-determination was to be the basis for settling territorial disputes. The League of Nations was to be the cornerstone of the peace, and Germany would be admitted at its inception. He did not intend to challenge Britain's domination of the seas, but wanted legal limits on it. The Alsace-Lorraine was to be unconditionally ceded to France (but just the Alsace-Lorraine, nothing more). The former German colonies would not be returned as long as Germany maintained its present political structure. Wilson also told Wiseman that he had no objection to an unofficial exchange of views among the Allies before the peace conference. He did not mention an indemnity or reparations, however, and wanted discussion of the Russian question put off until after the peace conference convened.[15]

At about this time, Allied intelligence sources revealed some unsettling news. Erich Ludendorff, it was discovered, had requested an armistice with the sole motive of keeping his army intact. When this was achieved, the liberal government would be dismissed.[16] The British passed on this information to Wilson, along with a copy of the German government's instructions to its minister in Tiflis (present-day Tbilisi) that ordered him to organize popular and "spontaneous" demonstrations, under German guidance, for self-determination, the outcome of which would be a regime friendly to Germany. These revelations again raised suspicions of possible German deceit. There were also reports, deliberately leaked by the Germans, that they intended to initiate a levee-en-masse and continue the fight if armistice terms were too hard. Perhaps the armistice demarche was a form of psychological warfare intended to demoralize the Allies; perhaps the German government was not serious about ending the war. It also became known in October that the chancellor had written a letter to his friend Prince Alexander von Hohenlohe in January 1918 in which he expressed his disdain for the Reichstag majority and for parliamentary democracy in general. This raised questions about the willingness of the German government to make political reforms. It was entirely conceivable that these matters, along with the sinking of the *Leinster*, led to the severer tone of Wilson's second note and might have persuaded him to impose conditions that the government of any sovereign state might find unacceptable.

But perhaps the rulers of Germany were not wholly in control of the political and social movements within their country as they had theretofore been. Intelligence and diplomatic sources reported growing political discontent in the Reich. Wherever there was social discontent, the possibility for Bolshevik exploitation of the situation weighed on the mind of the president and other Washington policymakers. It was conceivable that unconditional surrender would undermine the coalition government in Berlin and with it those who favored a negotiated peace; it would thereby either promote the success of the German militarists or the Bolsheviks, the former a despotism of the Right, the latter, a proletarian despotism. The prospects of either were sobering, if not frightening, in the view of moderates in the United States and England because the anarchy and terror that now reigned in Russia might spread to Central Europe. Lansing wrote on the 22nd that he fully expected a revolution in Germany. He hoped it would not be a Bolshevik revolution but nonetheless expressed satisfaction with the prospect that there might be a rapid political conclusion to a war at a time when a military conclusion did not appear to be in sight.[17]

Many within the ruling circles of Great Britain continued to rage over Wilson's handling of the correspondence with the Germans. Notwithstanding their indignation, they did realize that there existed a large body of opinion in Britain, even within the military, that favored pursuing an armistice. Wilson's second note, it was felt, had met the exacting standards the English themselves had set.[18] It would be politically unwise for the government to hinder Wilson's efforts, in view of this state of opinion. In France, public and parliamentary opinion was less critical of Wilson at this juncture. It is Arno Mayer's opinion that this was the case because, unlike Great Britain or the United States, no election was in the offing.

> [The] proximity of the battlefields, the staggering casualty figures, the devastation of the border provinces, and the economic and financial depletion made the French power elite particularly eager to avoid paying the extravagant cost of a final battle. . . . [The] generals and politicians alike were painfully aware of the large extent to which

France's own military stamina was dependent on American power. . . .
French military and Rightist circles confidently assumed that such an
agreement [i.e., an armistice that would paralyze Germany's military
strength] would so cripple Germany that she could not withstand
Carthaginian peace terms.[19]

Although the French were pleased by Wilson's position on the
Alsace-Lorraine, their political and military leaders were distinctly displeased
by the fact that the Germans had appealed to Wilson (and not to them), and
they were at least as uneasy as the British leaders were about his handling of
so important a matter as the prearmistice negotiations. In fact, many deputies
in the Chamber felt Wilson was pro-German. It is perhaps because
Clemenceau was so very much in control and had either the confidence or
could command the obedience of political and military authorities that there
were so few meetings of record called to discuss the question, and thus little
evidence of official criticism of the president. We may safely presume that an
ardent patriot like Clemenceau would want the strongest guarantees of French
security in any armistice and that an overwhelming majority of Frenchmen
trusted that he could and would obtain those guarantees. He had indeed
criticized the Fourteen Points in the press but had refrained from taking issue
with Wilson because he realized that achieving French security could best be
obtained with U.S. aid and by not antagonizing the president.

The Germans now, of course, had a crucial decision to make: to continue
dealing with the president or to break off talks regarding negotiations and
continue to fight. The government was in some disarray, as was public opinion. Most parties of the Right and the Military High Command now favored
breaking off talks. Wilson's second note, they felt, was an affront to Germany
and had dared to ask for too much. But the moderates and certainly the
parties of the Left argued that Germany should trust Wilson. The Social
Democrats declared that they would not support a peace acquired through
violence and humiliation, but they criticized the militarists in Germany who
were bent upon imperialistic conquest and who were opposed to the transformation of Germany into a democratic state. They also warned against irre-
sponsible agitation, for they too worried that the Bolsheviks or other social
revolutionaries could gain the upper hand in the event Germany fell into
chaos.

Prince Max decided against breaking off talks. He decided he would make
concessions on submarine warfare, with the emperor's reluctant approval, over
the opposition of the navy and Ludendorff, and prepared a reply to Wilson's
second note. On 20 October, the third German note was sent off to Wilson.
It protested against the reproach for alleged inhumane actions. German
troops were under the strictest instructions to spare private property and
exercise care, it declared, and those guilty of violating these instructions were

being punished. It denied that in the sinking of ships the German navy ever purposely destroyed lifeboats with their passengers and suggested that the facts of the cases be cleared up by neutral commissions. Orders had just been dispatched prohibiting further torpedoing of passenger shops in order to "avoid anything that might hamper the work of peace." With regard to the conditions of an armistice, the German government assumed "that the procedure of an evacuation and of the conditions of an armistice should be left to the judgement of the military advisers and that the actual standard of power on both sides in the field has to form the basis for arrangements safeguarding and guaranteeing this standard." The note asked the president to arrange the opportunity for fixing details of the armistice and evacuation, trusting that he would "approve of no demand which would be irreconcilable with the honor of the German people."[20]

With respect to the fundamental political condition of peace, the note declared that although hitherto the German people had not been given the power to influence the formation of a German government, a fundamental change had occurred: the present government, and henceforth all future governments, would be formed in accordance with the wishes of the people based upon equal, universal, secret, and direct franchise. Therefore, the offer of an armistice was legitimate, because it had been generated by a government that was supported by the majority of the German people.

Even with the concessions and the delineation of the government reforms undertaken by the German leaders, the Senate Republicans and the Allies continued to be skeptical and critical. The British foreign minister, Arthur Balfour, sent an urgent telegram to Lansing that pointed out that the Germans were seeking a "conditional armistice," assuming that only occupied territories would be evacuated, and would then set up a strong defense at their own frontiers. Balfour hoped the president would seek strong guarantees in an armistice in the event that negotiations break down. He hoped that no commitments would be made without consulting the Allies. In the House of Commons, the foreign secretary continued to be evasive about whether his government approved or disapproved of the Fourteen Points.

In the United States, the leaders of the Democratic party were worried about the effects of the concerted efforts against Wilson's handling of the correspondence with Germany. Anti-German sentiment in the country, they believed, was being harnessed by the Republicans to promote their campaign. Congressional elections were now less than three weeks away. The Democratic leaders became convinced that the president must make a public appeal to the U.S. people. The president was concerned that Republican opposition would hamper his current and future negotiations with Germany and would prevent him from working for the kind of peace he hoped for. He agreed to make a public statement urging the election of Democrats to Congress. On the 24th, Wilson made this appeal:

If you have approved of my leadership and wish me to continue to be your unembarrassed spokesman in affairs at home and abroad, . . . I earnestly beg that you will express yourselves unmistakably to that effect by returning a Democratic majority to both the Senate and the House of Representatives. . . . The return of a Republican majority to either house of Congress would . . . be interpreted on the other side of the water as a repudiation of my leadership.[21]

As we shall see, the Republicans accepted this challenge, and the appeal itself became a contested campaign issue.

Thus, fully aware of the political crosscurrents in the United States and, at least in general terms, the state of public opinion of the Allies, Wilson prepared the draft of a reply to the third German note. In a meeting at the White House on the 22nd, he discussed the situation with his cabinet. Among other things, the president expressed his fears about the spread of Bolshevism and the impact of the widespread hatred of the Germans in the country. The next day, he met with a smaller group of advisers (his war cabinet) and read them the reply he had prepared. As E. N. Hurley, chairman of the U.S. Shipping Board, wrote,

> Not a man present failed to realize that in that note Woodrow Wilson had written a declaration that would end the great World War. . . .
>
> [One] member believed it would be helpful from a political standpoint if a certain change were made in one expression. The President shook his head. . . . "No", he said decisively, "I am dealing in human lives—not in politics."[22]

This reply, sent off to the Swiss chargé d'affaires for transmission to the German government on 23 October, stated that the president "feels he cannot decline to take up with the Governments with which the Government of the United States is associated the question of an armistice" in view of the assurances and acceptance of the conditions by Germany. He had transmitted to the associated governments the correspondence between Germany and the United States:

> with the suggestion that, if those governments are disposed to effect peace upon the terms and conditions indicated, their military advisers and the military advisers of the United States be asked to submit . . . terms of such an armistice as will fully protect the interests of the peoples involved and ensure to the Associated Governments the unrestricted power to safeguard and enforce the details of the peace.

The note went on to recognize that constitutional changes brought about within Germany might be significant, but it did not "appear that the principle of a Government responsible to the German people has yet been fully worked out"; nor were there guarantees that these changes would be permanent. The German people had no means of commanding the military authorities of the empire, nor was the "power of the king of Prussia to control the policy of the Empire" impaired. The "determining initiative still remains with those who have hitherto been masters of Germany." The United States could deal with these "masters" only by demanding surrender, not offering peace negotiations. It would deal only with the "veritable representatives of the German people who have been assured of a genuine constitutional standing as the real rulers of Germany."[23]

Coincident with the dispatch of this note, Lansing forwarded the correspondence between the President and Germany to nineteen Allied countries, asking them to acquiesce in the course of action Wilson had pursued to that date and to take part in developing jointly the military terms of an armistice. He pointed out that the president had made every effort to safeguard the interests of the peoples with whom the United States was associated. France and Great Britain approved of this reply, and Clemenceau immediately set in motion the process for formulating Allied armistice terms.

In Germany, by the third week in October, Prince Max of Baden had reason to be concerned about the possibility of a revolt staged by the Army High Command. For the second time, the chancellor appeared before the Reichstag on the 22nd (his first appearance was on the 5th, when he notified the deputies that he had requested an armistice). He told them of the steps he had taken to liberalize the government. The Reichstag was deeply divided on governmental reforms, as it had been over the wisdom of proceeding with armistice negotiations. If Wilson's second note appeared to suggest to some that the kaiser must abdicate, the third note appeared even clearer on this issue. The Social Democrats and the more radical Independent Socialists favored abdication. The parties of the Right and Center were opposed to it. It was in these circumstances that, on 24 October, the High Command issued a defiant declaration to the troops, calling Wilson's reply a demand for unconditional surrender, which was unacceptable. The High Command appealed to the army to meet the challenge and continue resistance against the enemy. The chancellor regarded the action of the generals as unacceptable, even though he was thoroughly unhappy with Wilson's note. Certainly he did not favor abdication. Here he intended to temporize and face the issue much later, and then only if it were absolutely necessary. However, when Paul von Hindenburg and Ludendorff came to Berlin from Spa, in contravention of his explicit orders to the contrary, the chancellor decided to make these matters of confidence in his government. The appeal to the army and the generals' presence in Berlin could give the impression that the military leaders were still able to influence political decisions in Germany. Prince Max felt that this would undermine the assurances of governmental reform he had made in his note to President Wilson. On the issue, he won. The kaiser reluctantly dismissed Ludendorff (but not Hindenburg) on the 26th. On that day also, the German armies, defeated in Lorraine by U.S. forces, began a more or less orderly retreat to the Rhine.

The chancellor arranged for the drafting of a reply to Wilson's note of the 23rd. It was short. Dispatched on the 27th, it simply assured Wilson that negotiations were being conducted by a government representing the German people and that the military authorities were subject to this authority. Germany awaited "proposals for an armistice, which is the first step toward a peace of justice, as described by the President in his pronouncements."

A separate memorandum, handed to the Swiss government on the 28th for transmission to the president, described in greater detail the political reforms instituted by the German government: procedures for parliamentary votes of confidence in the chancellor, who was made fully responsible for all public statements of the kaiser; limitations on the Kaiser's rights as commander in chief of the armed forces; the institution of universal and equal suffrage by secret ballot in Prussia (which by then had been "definitively secured" but not yet implemented). The memorandum concluded with the observation that Germany had now joined the family of nations ruled by parliamentary governments in which "personal rule" by the monarch was no longer possible. This memorandum was not published in Germany, however, as was the reply of the 27th; nor indeed was it published in the United States after its receipt by the president. The secretary of state dismissed it as mere propaganda, as apparently did the president—although we cannot be sure of this. It is certain that he raised no objection of record to the decision *not* to publish it.[24]

Now whatever the actual political situation in Germany or the nature of the governmental crisis, Wilson could logically conclude that an armistice was possible. The president also had several sources of information about the policy of the Allies, including the cables from Colonel House, who arrived in Paris on the 26th. It is interesting to note that when the president sent off his confidant in mid-October, he told him, "I have not given you any instructions, because I feel you will know what to do."[25] Although House was given virtually no substantive instructions, he did carry a commission as "special representative of the United States in Europe in matters relating to the war" and was Wilson's "personal representative." He would therefore be privy to the most sensitive political and military matters and would take active part in the inter-Allied negotiations in the crucial weeks leading up to the armistice on 11 November.

Wilson was to learn early on that the Allies approved of his last note to the Germans, and he knew they were meeting in Paris to discuss procedures for the next diplomatic step (or steps) to be taken and, most important, the terms of the armistice. He presumed that he would receive a formal reply and proposals from them in the very near future. He learned on the 29th, from the Swedish minister in Washington, that Austria-Hungary had "accepted all the conditions which the President had put upon entering into negotiations on the subject of armistice and peace" and an immediate armistice on all Austro-Hungarian fronts."[26] Armed with the conviction that the Great War was at last ending, Wilson held a cabinet meeting on the 29th and, among other things, read aloud two cables he had received. The first was a plea for clemency from Heinrich Lammasch, the new Austrian prime minister, because (as the latter expressed it) of the existence of a new spirit in the German government. The second telegram, probably from the U.S. theologian George D. Herron, a friend of the president who lived in Geneva during the war, declared that the president need only give the word and the German people would overthrow the "Hohenzollern clique."[27] Wilson commented that he felt Germany should not be pushed too far because that would only increase the possibility of a Bolshevik revolution, and he did not want that to happen.

DISCUSSION QUESTIONS

1. *The president now needs an analysis of the steps the United States might propose to the Allies for the next phase of the move toward an armistice and peace settlement. What, in your view, can be done now and what are Wilson's sources of leverage over the Allies and the Germans?*
2. *What counterproposals are the Allies likely to make?*
3. *What instructions should Wilson telegraph to Colonel House?*

BREAKING THE DEADLOCK

Colonel House knew that his primary mission in Paris was to convince the Allies to accept the Fourteen Points as the basis for the peace settlement with Germany, preferably before the armistice was signed and hostilities ceased. The Germans had accepted them, and it was entirely possible that an Allied repudiation of Wilsonian principles would impel them to fight to the finish. Wilson had never abandoned his fixed purpose to make peace on the basis of his principles, no matter what language he employed in condemning Germany or its leaders. Colonel House understood this. The president had often discussed his goals with him during the war and even before, when he had sent his confidant to Europe on peace missions. House shared with the president the view that it was a matter of political necessity and indeed of honor to get the Allies to accept the Fourteen Points, even though, as victory approached, they might be less likely to accept being bound by them and having their freedom of action constrained. House expressed his fears that the Allies intended to wrest control of the peace negotiations from the president.

Now the Fourteen Points and the president's other principles were, of course, not without ambiguities. Nor was it known how they might be applied in the circumstances that prevailed after the fighting ended. The Allies criticized them variously as vague, utopian, and pro-German. Before their departure for Europe, House and Wiseman discussed Wilson's intentions and House gained a better understanding of the president's current interpretation of his principles of peace. But in order to better meet the criticisms of the Allies and to provide himself with more definite guidelines in the Paris negotiations, House asked Walter Lippmann and Frank I. Cobb, both liberal journalists (the latter was under consideration for the post of ambassador to Great Britain), to draft interpretive commentary on the Fourteen Points. The journalists completed their task, and their draft commentary was sent to Wilson on 29 October. Wilson's reply still left matters somewhat in the air: "Analysis of fourteen points satisfactory interpretation of principles involved but details of application mentioned should be regarded as merely illustrative suggestions and reserved for peace conference.[28] The president intended to preserve his freedom of action for the peace negotiations, which he had firmly made up his mind to attend himself. Believing, not without justification, that this reply constituted presidential approval, House proceeded to use the Lippmann-Cobb commentaries throughout the prearmistice negotiations as a standard reference, enabling him to reply to the Allies' questions. Unfortunately, German intelligence agencies intercepted and decoded them, and thus they were available to the German leaders no later than 2 November.[29] This confidential information provided the Germans with a blueprint of U.S. plans and motives. Wilson regarded Points 1, 2, 3, and 14 as the "essentially American" terms for peace.[30] Points 7 and 8 were of particular interest to France and Belgium, not only because of their reference to the evacuation of German forces and the territorial terms, but also because of their reference to war damages, which interested Great Britain as well. All these were the subject of intense discussion in the Paris meetings that House attended. They are listed below for reference, together with the Lippmann-Cobb interpretation.[31]

Point 1: Open covenants of peace, openly arrived at, after which there will be no private international Understandings of any kind, but diplomacy shall proceed always frankly and in public view.

LC: *The purpose is clearly to prohibit treaties or understandings that are secret, such as the [Triple Alliance], . . . etc.*

The phrase "openly arrived at" need cause no difficulty. In fact, the President explained to the Senate last winter that the phrase was not meant to exclude confidential diplomatic negotiations involving confidential matters. The intention is that nothing which occurs in the course of such confidential negotiations shall be binding unless it appears in the final covenant made public to the world.

The matter may perhaps be put this way: it is proposed that in the future every treaty be part of public law of the world, and that every nation assume a certain obligation in regard to its enforcement. Obviously, nations cannot assume obligations in matters of which they are ignorant; and therefore any secret treaty tends to undermine the solidarity of the whole structure of international covenants which it is proposed to erect.

Point 2: Absolute freedom of navigation upon the seas, outside territorial waters, except as the seas may be closed in whole or in part by international action for the enforcement of international covenants.

LC: *This proposition must be read in connection with number 14 which proposes a league of nations. It refers to navigation under the three following conditions: (1) general peace; (2) a general war, entered into by the League of Nations for the purpose of enforcing international covenants; (3) limited war, involving no breach of international covenants.*

Under "(1) General peace" no serious dispute exists. There is implied freedom to come and go [on the high seas].
No serious dispute exists as to the intention under "(2). . . ."
Obviously such a war is conducted against an outlaw nation and complete non-intercourse with that nation is intended.
"(3) A limited war . . ." is the crux of the whole difficulty. The question is, what are to be the rights of neutral shipping and private property on the high seas during a war between a limited number of nations when that war involves no issue upon which the League of Nations cares to take sides. In other words, a war in which the League of Nations remains neutral. Clearly, it is the intention of the proposal that in such a war the rights of neutrals shall be maintained against the belligerents, the rights of both to be clearly and precisely defined in the law of nations.

Point 3: The removal, so far as possible, of all economic trade barriers and the establishment of an equality of trade conditions among the nations consenting to the peace and associating themselves for its maintenance.

LC: *The proposal applies only to those nations which accept the responsibilities of membership in the League of Nations. It means the destruction of all special commercial agreements, each putting the trade of every other nation in the League on the same basis, the most-favored-nation clause applying automatically to all members of the League of Nations. Thus a nation could legally maintain a tariff or a special railroad rate or a port restriction against the whole world, or against all the signatory powers. It could maintain any kind of restriction which it chose against a nation not in the League. But it could not discriminate as between its partners in the League.*

This clause naturally contemplates fair and equitable understanding as to the distribution of raw materials.[32]

Point 7: Belgium, the whole world will agree, must be evacuated and restored without any attempt to limit the sovereignty which she enjoys in common with all free nations. No other single act will serve as this will serve to restore confidence among the nations in the laws which they have themselves set and determined for the government of their relations with one another. Without this healing act the whole structure and validity of international law is forever impaired.

LC: *The only problem raised here is in the word "restored". Whether restoration is to be in kind or how the amount of the indemnity is to be determined is a matter of detail, not of principle. The principle that should be established is that in the case of Belgium there exists no distinction between "legitimate" and "illegitimate" destruction. The initial act of invasion was illegitimate and therefore all the consequences of that act are of the same character. Among the consequences may be put the war debt of Belgium. The recognition of this principle would constitute "the healing act" of which the President speaks.*

Point 8: All French territory should be freed and the invaded portions restored, and the wrong done to France by Prussia in 1871 in the matter of Alsace-Lorraine, which has unsettled the peace of the world for nearly fifty years, should be righted in order that peace may once more be made secure in the interest of all.

LC: *In regard to the restoration of French territory, it might well be argued that the invasion of northern France, being the result of the illegal act as regards Belgium, was itself illegal. But the case is not perfect. As the world stood in 1914, war between France and Germany was not in itself a violation of international law, and great insistence should be put upon keeping the Belgian case dis-*

tinct and symbolic. Thus, Belgium might well, as indicated above, claim reimbursement not only for destruction but for the cost of carrying on the war. France could not claim payment, it would seem, for more than the damage done to her northeastern departments [the Alsace-Lorraine, French boundaries and Luxemburg].

Point 14: A general association of nations must be formed under special covenants for the purpose of affording mutual guarantees of political independence and territorial integrity to great and small [states] alike.

LC: *The principle of a league of nations as the primary essential of a permanent peace has been so clearly presented by President Wilson in his speech of September 27, 1918, that no further elucidation is required. It is the foundation of the whole diplomatic structure of a permanent peace.*

At the very first meeting between House and the Allied leaders on 29 October, the latter expressed doubts about "going in on the Fourteen Points." They did agree to review the points one by one, indicating that they would want to attach qualifications to them so that the Germans could have no doubts about the Allied position—assuming the Allies did accept them as the basis of the peace settlement. After the meeting, Colonel House sent a telegram to Lansing that summarized the results of the day's talks.[33] The French and Italian prime ministers, he said, were not at all in favor of the League of Nations, and the Italian minister intended to submit many objections to the Fourteen Points. Lloyd George still had problems about binding Great Britain to the president's principles and was especially vehement in his rejection of Point 2: "I do not wish to discuss it with Germany. I will not make it a condition of peace with Germany," he had said. The next day, House also learned that Clemenceau had prepared an elaborate brief that set forth his objections to the Fourteen Points.[34]

The often contentious discussions continued over the next several days, days in which the Allies also agreed upon armistice terms for Austria-Hungary and Turkey and continued to discuss the terms for Germany. The British continued to object to Point 2. Lloyd George would only agree to notifying the Germans that Britain would retain complete freedom on the subject of freedom of the seas when they entered the peace conference. At a conference on 3 November, House pressed the prime minister for acceptance of some compromise, as did Clemenceau. But Lloyd George replied:

No, it is impossible for any British Prime Minister to do this. It has got associated in the public mind with the blockade. It's no good saying I accept the principle. It would only mean that in a week's time a new Prime Minister would be here who would say that he could not accept the principle. The English people will not look at it. On this point the nation is absolutely solid. It's no use for me to say that I can accept when I know that I am not speaking for the British nation.[35]

The negotiations were complicated by yet another factor: the issue of damages, or what were later to be termed "reparations." The British submitted a memorandum on 30 October that, in effect, touched upon the interpretation of the word "restore" in Points 7 and 8. The Allied governments understood, it said, that Germany will make compensation "for all damage suffered by the civilian population of the Allies and by their property as the result of Germany's invasion of Allied lands, either on land, or on the sea, or in consequence of operations in the air."[36] On 1 November, France and Belgium urged that the armistice include terms for the restitution of their losses. The Belgian minister of foreign affairs, Paul Hymans, also asked for an interpretation of Point 3. Belgium wanted protection during reconstruction, he said, against German goods swamping its markets. Lloyd George asked whether Point 3 permitted any country to have preferential tariffs, whether Britain would be required to make an equal distribution of available stocks of raw materials among all peoples, and to what extent Germany would share in such a distribution. House admitted he could not answer these questions at this time. On 3 November Hymans raised the subject of restitution for damages once again, asking for a more ample interpretation of the phrase in the British memorandum of 30 October that would require Germany merely to make compensation for damages to civilian populations. When asked by Lloyd George whether he was asking for compensation for indirect damages, Hymans replied that he was not asking for it now, but that there should be a phrase in the text referring to it.

House pointed out that General Bliss had warned him that insistence on restitution at this time would entail great delays in the armistice negotiations. The subject ought more properly to be on the agenda of the peace conference. Clemenceau argued that the French people would demand an understanding on the matter. He urged that the principle of Germany's responsibility be recognized and proposed that a clause be inserted in the armistice terms to the following effect:

With the reservation that any future claims and demands of the Allies and the United States of America remain unaffected, the following financial conditions are required:
Reparation for damage done.
While the armistice lasts no public securities shall be removed by the enemy which can serve as a pledge to the Allies for the recovery or reparation of war losses. . . .

Restitution of the Russian and Roumanian gold yielded to the Germans or taken by that power.[37]

The publics of the Allies and the United States knew nothing of these disagreements on the principles of peace. It was certainly common knowledge that the Paris meetings were taking place and that the Allies were working to produce armistice terms for submission to Germany. In the period of the approximately ten days that passed after House's arrival in Paris and 5 November (the day of the congressional elections), U.S. newspapers and their readers were largely preoccupied with the great victories on the western front, the new Italian offensive against the Austrians, and the virtual collapse of the Austrian and Turkish armies as effective fighting forces. The Hapsburg monarchy was also disintegrating. On the 30th, Turkey accepted an armistice, and on 3 November, Austria-Hungary also accepted terms from General Pietro Badoglio of the Italian army on behalf of the Entente powers. By the 4th, Germany stood alone. Thus, publics everywhere could assume that the end of the war was near and that Germany itself would soon be given armistice terms.

In the last half of October, in addition to the news of the influenza pandemic, U.S. and foreign newspapers also reported on the political turmoil within Germany and of the possibility of the kaiser's abdication, although little was known of these matters in specific terms. Of the reforms that were reported, most newspapers, and certainly those of the Right, showed skepticism or distrust of their probable permanence. Most news about Germany, it turned out, was stale by about three to five days. However, with respect to the preoccupations of U.S. journalists and their readers, second only to news on the progress of the war was the subject of the midterm congressional elections, which would take place on 5 November. By all accounts, it was expected to be a very close election. The Republicans had reacted vigorously to the president's appeal to the U.S. people on 24 October, contending that Wilson was engaging in partisan politics and impugning the patriotism of the GOP. It was the Republicans, they maintained, who had prevailed against those Democrats in the East and North who had opposed preparedness before the war began; it was the Republicans who now stood for the complete defeat of the German enemy. As a party of high tariffs, they accused Wilson and the Democrats of supporting free trade that would bring grief to the U.S. economy. If Wilson's lenient peace plans were adopted, Germany, they declared, would be able to reap the fruits of free trade even though it was defeated. In late October, a group of Republican members of congress drafted a brief statement that proclaimed that they stood for protection, economic preparation for the peace, checking waste, and the pursuit of the war with greater vigor until Germany had unconditionally surrendered. They also pledged to support the Allies in their demand for reparation from the "accursed Huns."[38] The GOP campaigners criticized Wilson's diplomacy of the extended exchange of notes with Germany, and Senator Lodge and Theodore Roosevelt rejected all of Wilson's plans for a new international order. Senator Philander C. Knox declared that there would be no time to consider so dubious an enterprise as the League of Nations in the forthcoming peace negotiations; and Roosevelt, in a speech at Carnegie Hall, repudiated the Fourteen Points, which, he said, had been "greeted with enthusiasm by Germany and by all pro-Germans on this side of the water, especially by the Germanized Socialists and by the Bolsheviks of every grade.[39]

The Democratic leadership responded by defending Wilson's appeal. The crucial issue was leadership, they argued. The president had successfully led the country through the war and would shortly achieve peace. The choice was between a peace based on liberalism and justice, or imperialism, militarism, and standpattism. Everyone, except those who profited by the old order, wanted a reduction in armaments and a League of Nations. A Democratic Congress would sustain the president, who was the spokesman for liberals and progressives throughout the world.

In Great Britain, Labour and Radical party members asked the war cabinet to formally endorse Wilson's principles. However, the British government continued to be evasive about its intentions or its policy with respect to the Wilson program during questioning in the House of Commons, in spite of public and press support for it. A mass rally of the Labour party at Albert Hall on 3 October proclaimed support for Wilson, as had the Union for Democratic Control, which in meetings throughout the country vowed its resistance to the enlargement of demands upon Germany that might delay peace. The U.S. chargé d'affaires in London, Irwin B. Laughlin, reported at length on opinion in Great Britain. There was, he wrote on 29 October, a strong but numerically small party calling for unconditional surrender (the National party). He might well have added that it was a very vocal and widely publicized party. German reforms, Laughlin stated, were treated skeptically. Those within "higher official quarters" shrank from the idea of the kaiser's abdication because it was believed to be better to deal with a chastened emperor than an unknown quantity. "The country is more desirous of an early peace than it wishes to show." But the government was not likely, Laughlin felt, to recant any stated war aims because these had become firmly implanted in the public mind. They would probably be willing to forgo a dictated peace or humiliating Germany, but the nation would not shrink from continuing the war should that be necessary. "[Should] an early peace prove to be unobtainable the general disappointment will be far more keen than will be immediately apparent, and the natural reaction might weaken the morale of the country."[40]

In France, Socialists and the large labor organizations sought to pressure the government into accepting Wilson's principles. They feared that the government and the parties of the Right intended not only to secure a punitive peace against Germany, but also to maximize French territorial acquisitions, increase French influence in Eastern Europe, and suppress socialism in Russia. But neither their press, nor their interpellations in the Chamber of Deputies, succeeded in persuading Clemenceau to make a commitment to a Wilsonian program. The premier made no public comment and his agents in the Chamber succeeded in quashing effective challenges on grounds that it might create the impression that there were differences between Wilson and the Allies.[41] Clemenceau, his supporters, and the parties of the Right, it appeared, were not to be deterred from their search for an armistice and peace settlement guarantees of "adequate security" for France, either by the reforms that had been undertaken in Germany or even by the threat of Bolshevism—in Germany or France. Indeed, the premier (joined on this point by Giorgio Sonnino of Italy) believed that Germany was playing on Allied fears of Bolshevism in order to win easy terms.

Wilson's principles had wide support in Italy, although the Italian leaders were more interested in the settlement with Austria-Hungary and fulfillment of the terms of the Treaty of London of 1916. They insisted secretly on reservations to the Fourteen Points that would enhance their claims on the eastern littoral of the Adriatic and in Trentino. There was, however, wide public support for Wilson's program in Italy insofar as the public understood it.

DISCUSSION QUESTIONS

1. *The president calls you in on the morning of 5 November, Election Day. He reviews the facts as presented previously. He tells you that he is determined to implement his peace plan and insists that in spite of the very great complexities of the international situation, he wants the Fourteen Points and his other principles to be the basis of a peace settlement with Germany. First, he asks you to review the arguments both for and against pursuing his path of principle. Then he asks you to suggest the alternatives open to him in dealing with the Allies over this question.*
    a. *What leverage does he have?*
    b. *How should he use it?*
    c. *What paths of compromise exist?*
    d. *Is there an interpretation of the points in contention that might be the basis of a compromise (without vitiating their meaning)?*
2. *He also asks you to consider the possible impact on these questions of a Democratic defeat at the polls today. (But he emphasizes again that his principles will be the basis of a U.S. peace with Germany as long as he is*

president.) After you have met his requests, he will prepare instructions to send to Colonel House in Paris.

3. *How did the dominant U.S. role at the end of the war influence the direction of the talks? How has Wilson's strict adherence to moral principles and the conditions of the Fourteen Points facilitated or obstructed a settlement in this case?*

NOTES

1. *Papers Relating to the Foreign Relations of the United States, 1918, Supplement I, The World War* (Washington, DC: Government Printing Office, 1933), pp. 12-17, hereinafter cited as "FRUS."

2. *Ibid.*, pp. 108-113.

3. *Ibid.*

4. *Ibid.*, pp. 309-310.

5. *Ibid.*, pp. 316-321, at p. 319.

6. *Ibid.*, p. 337.

7. *Ibid.*, p. 343.

8. Quoted from Ludendorff's memoirs by Harry R. Rudin, *Armistice 1918* (New Haven, CT: Yale University Press, 1944), p. 103.

9. FRUS, p. 357-358.

10. Arno J. Mayer, *Politics and Diplomacy of Peacemaking: Containment and Counterrevolution at Versailles, 1918-1919* (New York: Alfred A. Knopf, 1967), p. 57.

11. Rudin, *Armistice 1918*, p. 126.

12. FRUS, p. 337.

13. Klaus Schwabe, *Woodrow Wilson, Revolutionary Germany, and Peacemaking, 1918-1919*, translated from German by Rita and Robert Kimber (Chapel Hill: University of North Carolina Press, 1985), p. 53.

14. FRUS, p. 368.

15. Schwabe, *Woodrow Wilson*, pp. 81-82; and Arthur C. Walworth, *America's Moment: 1918* (New York: Norton, 1977), pp. 23-24.

16. FRUS, p. 374.

17. *Ibid.*, p. 63.

18. Rudin, *Armistice 1918*, p. 137.

19. Mayer, *Politics and Diplomacy of Peacemaking*, p. 85.

20. FRUS, pp. 380-381.

21. *New York Times*, 26 October 1918.

22. Rudin, *Armistice 1918*, p. 171.

23. FRUS, pp. 381-383.

24. Schwabe, *Woodrow Wilson*, p. 99 and note 100 on p. 434. See also pp. 73 and 75.

25. Ray Stannard Baker, *Woodrow Wilson: Life and Letters* (Garden City, NY: Doubleday, Page & Co., 1939), vol. 8, p. 477.

26. FRUS, pp. 404-405.

27. Schwabe, *Woodrow Wilson*, p. 72. See pp. 24ff. for additional information on Herron and other U.S. sources of information on events occurring within Germany.

28. FRUS., p. 421.

29. Schwabe, *Woodrow Wilson*, p. 110.

30. FRUS, p. 428.

31. *Ibid.*, pp. 405-413.

32. See Walworth, *America's Moment*, pp. 66-67 for Wilson's letter to Senator Furnifold M. Simmons expatriating on the meaning of Point 3. *New York Times*, 29 October 1918, published the explanation.

33. FRUS, pp. 421-423.

34. *Ibid.*, p. 425.

35. *Ibid.*, p. 456.

36. FRUS, pp. 425-427.

37. *Ibid.*, p. 466. The section in the clause about restitution of Russian and Romanian gold refers to the gold indemnity received by the Germans after the signing of the peace treaties of Brest-Litovsk (March 1918) and Bucharest (May 1918), with the Russian Bolshevik regime and with Romania.

38. Mayer, *Politics and Diplomacy of Peacemaking*, p. 126.

39. *Ibid.*, p. 127.

40. FRUS, pp. 413-415.

41. Mayer, *Politics and Diplomacy of Peacemaking*, p. 86.

FURTHER READING ON WORLD WAR I

Gelfand, Lawrence E. *The Inquiry: American Preparations for Peace, 1917-1919.* New Haven: Yale University Press, 1963.

Kennan, George F. *The Decision to Intervene.* Princeton: Princeton University Press, 1956.

Link, Arthur S. *Wilson the Diplomatist.* Baltimore: Johns Hopkins University Press, 1957.

Mayer, Arno J. *Politics and Diplomacy of Peacemaking: Containment and Counterrevolution at Versailles, 1918-1919.* New York: Alfred A. Knopf, 1967.

Papers Relating to the Foreign Relations of the United States, 1918, Supplement I, The World War. Washington, DC: Government Printing Office, 1933.

Rudin, Harry R. *Armistice 1918*. New Haven, CT: Yale University Press, 1944.

Schmitt, Bernadotte E., and Harold C. Vedeler. *The World in the Crucible: 1914-1919*. New York: Harper and Row, 1984.

Schwabe, Klaus. *Woodrow Wilson, Revolutionary Germany, and Peacemaking, 1918-1919*. Chapel Hill: University of North Carolina Press, 1985.

Shaw, Albert. *President Wilson's State Papers and Addresses*. New York: George H. Doran Co., 1917.

Ullman, Richard. *Intervention and the War*. Princeton: Princeton University Press, 1961.

Walworth, Arthur C. *America's Moment: 1918*. New York: Norton and Co., 1977.

3

■ ══════════════════════════════════════ ■

CONCLUDING THE WAR
OVER SUEZ, 1956

The crisis began with President Abdal Nasser's decision to nationalize the Suez Canal, which he announced on 26 July 1956. That decision followed the news, that John Foster Dulles, the U.S. secretary of state, had transmitted to the Egyptian ambassador on 19 July that the United States would not help fund the construction of the Aswan High Dam. Britain joined the United States in that decision. British prime minister Sir Anthony Eden blamed Nasser for the recent dismissal of Glubb Pasha from the command of the Jordanian army and behaved in an openly hostile manner toward Nasser. U.S., British, and French leaders had also concluded, in March 1956, that Nasser's stature as an Arab leader should be diminished. They differed substantially, however, over the degree to which this should be accomplished by force rather than by diplomacy.

REACHING THE DECISION TO NEGOTIATE

The Egyptian takeover of the Suez Canal was completed without bloodshed. Egypt offered compensation. Western pilots were retained, and the canal continued to operate efficiently. Furthermore, Nasser's act of nationalization, though unilateral and preemptive, was not illegal and was not a violation of international law. Although Egypt had nationalized the Suez Canal Company and its assets, the company was conceived as a temporary concession operating on Egyptian soil, which would be dissolved in 1968, at

---

This chapter is an edited version of the case study by Michael G. Fry, The Suez Crisis, 1956, *Pew case study no. 126.*

which time management of the company's operations would revert to Egypt. Nasser had not committed an act of aggression; he had simply accelerated the transfer process. Technically, the canal company was Egyptian and subject to Egyptian law. In one sense, the only issue was whether Nasser had violated the Constantinople Convention of 1888 and infringed upon the maritime rights of the international community. The convention guaranteed unrestricted passage through the canal and set conditions for international usage of the canal.

Middle Eastern stability was a primary consideration of many Western nations. Apparent Soviet attempts to force Iran, Turkey and Greece into its orbit of influence prompted the United States to respond with the Truman Doctrine of 1947. In 1950, France, Britain, and the United States formed the Tripartite Pact, pledging to constrain the Middle East arms race, to regulate the flow of arms to Israel and the Arab states on the basis of need, to prevent the violation of the 1949 armistice agreements, and to aid any victim of aggression. In 1955, the Baghdad Pact was signed by Iraq, Turkey, Iran, Pakistan, and Britain in an attempt to provide a system of regional security and to contain Soviet influence. The Soviet Union saw the signing of the pact as a hostile act, Egypt saw it as elevating Iraq to the level of regional leader and Egyptian rival, France saw it as an insult, and Israel saw it as a threat to its security. As events unfolded in response to the Baghdad arrangement, the Soviets began to supply weapons to Egypt, and France chose to furnish arms to Israel. At this point, however, Nasser still relied on Western economic aid and investment. Consequently the Aswan High Dam project became the central issue in Egyptian relations with the West.

The Egyptian position was both anti-imperialist and anti-British, reflecting the resentment of former British colonial control. Although the first Anglo-Egyptian treaty of 1936 recognized Egyptian independence, it also provided for British occupation of military bases in the Suez Canal zone. As a result of Egyptian antagonism and nationalism, a new treaty was concluded in 1954, which promised evacuation of all British forces from the Canal Zone in return for the British option to maintain the defense of forces in the Middle East. Unfortunately, Nasser was not content with the terms of the 1954 treaty and pursued wider dreams of regional arrangements based on Egyptian dominance. Egyptian aspirations added a new dimension to inter-Arab relations and precipitated various international reactions.

France saw the act of nationalization as an opportunity to be exploited—as a chance to damage Nasser's prestige in Egypt, the Arab world, and the nonaligned movement, to end Egyptian support for the Algerian revolt, and, perhaps, to bring Nasser down. Destroying Nasser would eliminate the principal destabilizing force in the Middle East and North Africa and help secure France's preeminent position in Algeria. The French government would accomplish these goals through diplomacy if possible, but by force if necessary. The French seemed to find little reason to encourage or support a peaceful resolution of the affair and seemed actually to prefer a military solution. France could assume, with some confidence, that its dubious image in Britain would be transformed overnight and that Britain would be anxious to act with France against Egypt. On 29 July, Christian Pineau, the French foreign minister, went to London to develop a joint Anglo-French plan of action against Nasser, which suggested that French forces and facilities would be placed under British command as part of a military plan.

The British, angry at Nasser's "theft" and similarly aware that Nasser had not violated international law, decided to build a case around the popular principle of internationalization. They maintained that the rights of the user states could only be guaranteed by international management and control of the canal, that the canal could not be subject to the politics of any one nation, including Egypt, and that Egypt apparently could not operate the canal efficiently. Furthermore, the British government decided to pursue these objectives through either the threat of force or actual military operations, even without U.S. or French assistance. Britain's position in the Middle East and as a world power were seen to be at stake. In the British view, the use of force was justified in defense of legitimate and vital national interests. The Suez Canal has been traditionally viewed as the "jugular vein" of the British system of influence in the Middle East and vital to the protection of their regional economic interests in areas of oil production, trade, investment, communication, and transportation. In addition, they perceived Nasser as a Soviet client and as a threat to the pro-Western Arab states and, accordingly, sought to restrain his ambitions.

Soviet motives in the Middle East were clear: to reduce Western influence in the region and to further expand Soviet leverage through a policy of military and economic aid to key Arab states and through opposition to the Baghdad Pact. As in any Middle East crisis, the Soviet Union perceived an opportunity to exploit the situation by encouraging the anti-Western and anticolonial sentiments of the Arab states. Perpetuation of the dispute would be to Soviet advantage.

The U.S. position was initially decided by President Dwight Eisenhower and Secretary of State Dulles. They concluded that Nasser had acted legally, if badly, and that a firm attitude must be adopted in order to assure compliance with the 1888 convention. International involvement in the canal's management and operation was preferable, if it was consistent with Egyptian sovereignty. But the president did not feel that there was a basis for military action. Eisenhower and Dulles searched for a policy designed to solve a variety of Middle East problems in a manner that secured regional peace and stability, furthered U.S. interests, and limited Soviet involvement. In response to the current Middle East situation, Eisenhower and Dulles chose to pursue a strategy designed to limit Nasser's influence in the region yet retain an option of returning to the Western camp. They hoped to find a way to balance between Israel's security needs and Arab aspirations, and they were determined to protect Western Europe's oil supplies without underwriting British and French imperial policies. Consequently, a negotiated settlement was a priority and diplomacy must not serve as a mere preface to the use of force. The British attitude was judged unwise. It was regarded as a threat to economic stability, oil supplies, and peace and out of step with contemporary beliefs and trends. It would also play into Soviet hands. This message was taken to London by Dulles and provided the basis for his position in discussions there from 1 to 3 August. But this posture was accompanied by Dulles's statement to Eden that Nasser must disgorge what he was attempting to swallow, a view shared by Eisenhower, but only in the sense of creating an international regime for the canal and thus ameliorating the impact of nationalization. Eisenhower did not want Nasser's leadership and actual position challenged on the canal issue.

Although their motives differed, France, Britain, and the United States jointly called for an international conference to convene in London on 16 August in an attempt to initiate multilateral negotiations outside of the U.N. Twenty-two powers attended the London Conference, including eight parties to the 1888 convention and sixteen maritime nations. Nasser rejected an invitation to participate. A set of proposals was adopted, with the Soviet bloc casting the only negative votes. The resulting Eighteen Power Proposal was presented to Nasser on 2 September, linked with threats of force to guarantee acceptance by Egypt. However, Nasser was unimpressed by the threats and refused to agree to international control of the canal. He chose instead to assert Egyptian independence and demonstrate firm Arab leadership. Thus the proposals and negotiations ultimately failed.

Eighteen Power Proposal

1. Representatives of the 18 governments who joined in the proposals which were subsequently submitted to the Egyptian Government by the Five Nation Committee presided over by the Prime Minister of Australia, the Right Honorable Robert Menzies, as a basis for negotiating a settlement of the Suez Canal question, met in London from 19-21 September, 1956. The purpose was to consider the situation in the light of the report of that Committee and other developments since the first London Conference.
2. They noted with regret that the Egyptian Government did not accept these proposals and did not make any counter-proposals to the Five Nation Committee.
3. It is the view of this Conference that these proposals still offer a fair basis for a peaceful solution of the Suez Canal problem, taking into account the

interests of the user nations as well as those of Egypt. The 18 Governments will continue their efforts to obtain such a settlement. The proposal made by the Egyptian Government on 10 September was placed before the Conference, but it was considered too imprecise to afford a useful basis for discussion.

4. A declaration was drawn up providing for the establishment of a Suez Canal Users Association. This Association is designed to facilitate any steps which may lead to a final or provisional solution of the Suez Canal problem. It will further co-operation between the Governments adhering to it, concerning the use of the Canal. For this purpose it will seek the co-operation of the competent Egyptian authorities pending a solution of the larger issues. It will also deal with such problems as would arise if the traffic through the Canal were to diminish or cease. The Association will be established as a functioning entity at an early date after the Delegates to this Conference have had an opportunity to consult in relation thereto with their respective Governments.

5. The Conference noted that on 12 September, 1956, the Governments of the U.K. and France informed the Security Council of the United Nations of the situation, and that subsequently, on 17 September, the Government of Egypt also made a communication to the Security Council. The Conference considers that recourse should be had to the United Nations whenever it seems that this would facilitate a settlement.

6. The Representatives of the 18 Governments have found their co-operation at the Conference valuable and constructive. The 18 Governments will continue to consult together in order to maintain a common approach to the problems which may arise out of the Suez question in the future.

7. It is the conviction of the Conference that the course outlined in this statement is capable of producing by peaceful means a solution which is in conformity with the principles of justice and international law as declared in Article I of the Charter of the United Nations.

On 10 September Nasser announced that he would pursue a peaceful settlement consistent with Egypt's sovereignty. He proposed, to the secretary-general of the U.N., a fresh round of multilateral negotiations by representatives of the user states in a newly formed "negotiating body," presumably a conference. Britain and France now had the following options: initiating multilateral negotiations with Egypt, submitting the dispute to the United Nations for mediation, adopting the Dulles plan to craft an international regime for the Canal, and using force. Their ability to activate any of these options depended to a significant degree on the attitude of the United States.

DISCUSSION QUESTIONS

1. *What are the costs and benefits associated with each of these options?*
2. *How could Nasser counter them?*
3. *Why was U.S. leverage critical to the effectiveness of the options?*
4. *What assumptions about each course of action are the principal parties making?*

GETTING TO THE TABLE

Britain and France had no difficulty in evading Nasser's call for negotiations of 10 September. Key regional and European powers ignored the initiative, although Ceylon, Indonesia, Pakistan, Spain, and the Soviet Union welcomed it. Eisenhower dismissed it as irrelevant.

The United Nations option had been there from the start. Those who rendered advice to Britain (Canada for example) urged that it be given priority during August and early September. Submitting the dispute to the U.N. was viewed as a strategy to secure international support and demonstrate the legality of the Anglo-French position. The French government was not as sanguine and reacted in a decidedly lukewarm manner to the U.N. option. Realistically, there were grounds to be cautious. The Soviet Union would veto both an anti-Egyptian strategy in the Security Council and measures to implement it. In the General Assembly, Britain and France would face Afro-Asian and Communist bloc votes and more negative propaganda. The procedures and powers of both the Security Council and the General Assembly might not operate in their favor, and that pointed to a further dilemma. If Britain and France did not go to the U.N., then Egypt might pursue this course with Soviet support and win the support of the General Assembly. When Canada urged Britain to put the dispute to the Security Council, Canada did so on the assumption that such a step would be endorsed by the United States and contribute both to Anglo-American cooperation and Western solidarity. This assumption proved unfounded. Eden had concluded that the best strategy would be to submit the dispute to the Security Council. But that step could be taken only after Britain had received U.S. assurances that there would be no deviation from the proposals to bring about international control of the canal and that the United States would vote against any resolution to eliminate the use of force. Dulles refused to give such assurances.

This Anglo-American disagreement regarding activation of the U.N. option in mid-September reflected their differing, fundamental assumptions and indicated the potential that existed for a very serious disagreement between them. Eisenhower and Dulles were determined to find a peaceful settlement. They assumed that prolonged negotiations would undermine the case for and reduce the possibility of a resort to force. Negotiations were meant to produce a settlement. Eden saw negotiations, coupled with economic and financial sanctions and the much-publicized military buildup, as a way to assert pressure on Nasser. They were to be a vindication of the legal and moral validity of the Anglo-French case. They could serve as a preface to the use of force. Eisenhower wanted delay, whereas Eden wanted prompt and determined action.

On 4 September, Dulles unveiled a provisional, scarcely thought-through scheme whereby the users would organize themselves into a "club" in order to exercise their rights under the 1888 convention. They would hire pilots, supervise operations, organize traffic, and collect tolls to be used to operate and improve the canal and compensate Egypt for the facilities provided to the users, all in cooperation with Egypt. This scheme would buy time to find common ground between Britain, France, and Egypt and prevent the use of force. The canal dispute was not the issue on which to bring Nasser down. A resort to force would, in the long term, destroy Western influence in the Middle East and provide a golden opportunity for the Soviet Union. Perhaps Dulles thought that operation of the canal would revert to the users' association if Egypt found it impossible to operate the canal efficiently or interfered with the users' rights. Eden found Dulles's proposal singularly unimpressive and unrealistic but embraced it in order to prevent the continued payment of tolls to Egypt and to increase the possibility of a breach of the 1888 convention by Egypt through a confrontation over the management of the canal. Such a confrontation might provide the legal and moral basis and increase the likelihood of U.S. support for sterner measures by the users, including force against Egypt. On 12 September, Eden presented the plan for a Suez Canal Users Association (SCUA) to Parliament in stern and uncompromising language along with threats of additional steps and possible unilateral action. Guy Mollet, the French prime minister, followed suit on 13 September. On 13 September, Dulles endorsed the SCUA plan as an interim arrangement but made it very clear that the United States did "not intend to shoot our way through." If Nasser refused transit to ships under the SCUA plan, the United States would not support measures to force passage through the canal; U.S. shipping to Europe would take the Cape route.

Without due regard for Dulles's sensitivities and preferences, Britain and France, on 23 September, requested the U.N. Security Council to meet on 26 September to consider the unilateral actions of Egypt, which, they asserted, threatened users' rights under the 1888 convention. Dulles was intensely irritated by the step and judged it to be a mistake. Egypt countered on 24

September, asking the Security Council to examine the actions of certain powers, particularly Britain and France, which threatened international peace. As a result of Egypt's continued refusal to allow Israeli ships to use the canal, on 26 September Israel attempted to secure a role in the U.N. negotiations scheduled for 5 October. The Israeli strategy was unsuccessful. Soviet foreign minister Nikolay Bulganin informed Eden, on 28 September, that the SCUA violated the 1888 convention and threatened Egypt's sovereign rights. He warned that military threats and the attempt to interfere in Egypt's domestic affairs could jeopardize the peace. Bulganin's initiative was only one of the signs that the Anglo-French initiative at the U.N. was likely to fail. The threat of the use of force had begun to alienate the Latin American states. The Afro-Asian states were warming to Nasser, the defiant underdog who was standing heroically against the white imperialists. But Eden had gone to the U.N. to secure nothing less than what Nasser had already rejected, which was the essence of the Eighteen Power proposals of August. Failing that, force would be used. Eden made some effort to convince Eisenhower that Soviet policy was the real danger, that Nasser was in Soviet hands, just as Benito Mussolini had been in Adolf Hitler's, and that it would be an error to appease him. French leaders, skeptical about the SCUA scheme and impatient with but acquiescing in the approach to the Security Council, were convinced that force would have to be used, and promptly. They had little faith in the United States. They felt that Egypt and the Soviet Union would be the only beneficiaries of further delay. On 28 September, Golda Meir, the Israeli foreign minister, and Moshe Dayan, chief of staff, were received in Paris. Plans were discussed further for an Israeli-French attack on Egypt in mid-October.

Dulles and Eisenhower knew nothing of these military conversations between France and Israel and, in any case, faced other complications. Dulles, on 2 October, publicly confirmed his attachment to the SCUA plan but emphasized its voluntary nature and the need to bargain with Egypt over its implementation. There could be no question of forcing Egypt to comply. In the same statement, he distanced the United States from the policies of both the colonial powers, Britain and France, and those excessively exuberant states seeking their complete and immediate independence. Decolonization must come, but in an evolutionary, constructive, and nonviolent way. Having angered Britain and France once more, Dulles, in private discussions with Baron John Selwyn-Lloyd and Pineau, attempted to construct an Anglo-American-French joint position as a preface to the deliberations of the Security Council. It seemed necessary to reassure France and Britain, who were complaining of the lack of U.S. support. They had reason to complain. But Eisenhower wanted to preserve an independent posture and retain certain open lines to Egypt.

The Security Council began its work on 5 October. Britain and France, predictably, would settle for nothing less than the Eighteen Power proposals. Dulles endorsed those proposals, sympathizing with the Anglo-French predicament, but he spoke of flexibility, of various possible ways to implement their essential principles. The Security Council must be creative. There could be no ultimatum to Egypt.

Mahmoud Fawzi, the Egyptian foreign minister, was also rhetorically moderate and flexible. Egypt, Fawzi stated, was willing to participate in a small negotiating group to seek agreement on principles providing for the guarantee of free transit, cooperation between the users and the Egyptian authorities running the canal, the setting of fair tolls, the settling of disputes, and the establishment of measures to develop and improve the canal. This looked promising. On the evening of 9 October, Lloyd, Pineau, and Fawzi began their private discussions, under the eye of Dag Hammarskjöld, the secretary-general of the U.N. They were to clarify Egypt's position and find a basis for further negotiations by agreeing on the principles that would underpin a settlement. They were not expected to produce a final settlement at these sessions, yet substantial progress was made. On the evening of 12 October, Hammarskjöld gave to the press and the Security Council a statement of their six principles for a settlement. They were vague and included no plan for implementation.

The Six Principles

1. There shall be free and open transit throughout the canal without discrimination, overt and covert.
2. Egypt's sovereignty shall be respected.
3. The operation of the canal shall be insulated from the politics of any country.
4. The manner of fixing tolls and charges shall be decided by agreement between Egypt and the users.
5. A fair proportion of the dues shall be allotted to development.
6. In case of dispute, unresolved affairs between The Suez Canal Company and the Egyptian government shall be settled by arbitration with suitable terms of reference and suitable provisions for the payment of sums found to be due.

Lloyd and Pineau adhered to the Eighteen Power Proposal, which provided for international control of the operation and management of the canal as the basis of any future negotiations. They called on Fawzi to propose precise ways to apply the Six Principles and bridge their differences.

At the Security Council on 13 October, that part of an Anglo-French resolution embodying the Six Principles was adopted unanimously. But Egypt objected to it and the U.S.S.R. vetoed the section of the resolution that identified the Six Principles with the Eighteen Power Proposal and described the latter as the basis for future negotiations. This resolution disregarded the concessions made by Egypt. The Security Council resolution also asked Egypt to propose precise ways to implement the Six Principles and guarantee users' rights, and it proposed interim cooperation between the SCUA and the Egyptian Canal Board to operate the canal. This section was endorsed by a 9 to 2 vote. The next step seemed to be for Fawzi and Hammarskjöld to produce proposals for a resumption of the bargaining, perhaps in Geneva, on 29 October.

Britain and France, however, made no effort to join in further negotiations with Egypt. The United States, the Soviet Union, Canada, and India were left virtually in the dark to ponder the implications of mounting tension on the Israeli-Jordan border, of Israeli military preparations aided by France, of spotty intelligence reports, of Iraqi efforts to stave off disintegration in Jordan (Jordan's elections were held on 21 October) brought about by pro-Egyptian factions, and of a further incident between France and Egypt over alleged arms shipments to Algeria. Continued discussions on the SCUA were irrelevant. Fawzi and Hammarskjöld appeared to have made progress in their consultations by 23 October, and the secretary-general called for a resumption of tripartite discussions in Geneva on 29 October. He received no response from London or Paris.

DISCUSSION QUESTIONS

1. *Which of the parties to the conflict had decided to negotiate at this point? Which had not?*
2. *Were all using the term "negotiation" in the same manner?*
3. *What alternative to the use of force could have been proposed by the United States at this point? Should public or private diplomacy have been used?*

BREAKING THE DEADLOCK

On 14 October, Albert Gazier, France's acting foreign minister, and General Maurice Challe, the deputy chief of staff, arrived in London to discuss ways to implement the option of force in order to regain control of the canal and to remove Nasser. The preferred plan pointed to an Israeli attack on Egypt and Anglo-French intervention as peacemakers by way of an ultimatum, bombing whichever side rejected it (i.e., Egypt), and then occupying the Canal Zone. On 15 October, Lloyd and Pineau returned to Europe from New York. On 16 October, Eden, Lloyd, Mollet, and Pineau met in Paris to evaluate the situation and review the military options. Eden was anxious to be "caught by surprise" by an Israeli attack on Egypt and to avoid direct collusion with Israel. Britain would continue to protect Jordan. David Ben-Gurion, Israel's prime minister, learned of the proposed scheme to activate the military option on 14 October; he denounced it as a typical piece of British perfidy. He was deeply concerned, understandably, about the Anglo-French discussions and immediately pressed the French to make the secret discussions tripartite. Israel must be an equal partner. Ben-Gurion valued the close ties with France and the supply of arms. He saw the opportunity that was unfolding for Israel, despite his dislike of the proposed plan for attacking Egypt.

The French invited Ben-Gurion to come to Paris; he arrived in the suburb of Sèvres on 22 October. The French asserted less-than-subtle pressure on Ben-Gurion as a preface to Lloyd's arrival that evening. The deal was struck and recorded in a formal, signed agreement on 24 October—the Sèvres Protocol. Eden was furious that a record of the collusion existed and attempted to retrieve the document. Ben-Gurion had negotiated certain minor amendments: Anglo-French air strikes against Egypt would come forty-eight hours (not seventy-two hours) after the Israeli attack, the French would provide an air defense against Egyptian bomber attacks on Israeli cities, and Britain agreed to restrain Jordan and Iraq from attacking Israel. However, the essence of the Anglo-French plan remained. Israel would attack in the Sinai. Britain and France would issue an ultimatum to both sides, bomb Egyptian airfields, and then intervene between the belligerents by occupying the Canal Zone. All that remained of the plan was to conceal the agreement, particularly from the United States (to deflect Eisenhower's pressure on Ben-Gurion) and to put the scheme into effect.

The military events unfolded rapidly. The Israeli attack on Egypt, launched on 29 October, was a spectacular success. Israeli forces were in command of the Sinai by 2 November. On 30 October, Britain and France issued their discriminatory ultimatum to Egypt and Israel, and on 31 October, they bombed Egyptian airfields. On 4 November, Egypt sank ships in, and thereby blocked, the Suez Canal. On 5 November, British and French paratroops were dropped at Port Said and Port Fuad, at the north end of the canal. On 6 November, the Anglo-French seaborne invasion force landed at Port Said, and then Britain, France, and Israel agreed to a cease-fire. On 7 November, Middle East time, the cease-fire went into effect.

The diplomatic events also unfolded at a rapid pace. The United States was involved in the final week of the election campaign. News of the Israeli attack reached Washington in the late afternoon of 29 October; Eisenhower convened a strategy session that evening. Though suspicious of Britain and France, and fearing their intentions, Eisenhower decided to declare his intention to honor the U.S. obligation to aid the victim of aggression under the Tripartite Pact. The United States would—with British and French support, it hoped—condemn Israel's aggression at the Security Council. On 30 October, Eisenhower, knowing now that Britain and France would not cooperate in the Security Council, also faced the evidence of the Anglo-French ultimatum, strong suspicion of the Anglo-French-Israeli collusion, and entirely unconvincing explanations from Eden. Eisenhower put the issue to the Security Council: He was undeterred and determined to prevent escalation of the conflict, Soviet mischief, and an outburst of Arab anti-Western anger. He was determined to uphold the U.N. Charter, to save Britain and France from their folly, and to limit damage to the Western alliance. He was also bent on using the crisis to find a settlement for the canal question and the Arab-Israeli dispute. But the Security Council was handcuffed, on 30 and 31 October, by Anglo-French vetoes of U.S. and U.S.S.R. resolutions calling for a cease-fire, Israeli withdrawal, and nonintervention by any power, i.e., the providing of arms. Australia stood by Britain and France. Thus the issue went to the General Assembly on 1 November, under the Uniting for Peace procedures. The United States, as Dulles told the National Security Council on 1 November, would stand on principle and against imperialism.

Combined Canadian and U.S. initiatives, from 1 to 4 November, with Lester Pearson more visible but Dulles more influential, and Hammarskjöld initially skeptical, produced the resolution, which Pearson skillfully introduced and linked to the Afro-Asian resolution proposed by India. Both resolutions were adopted by the General Assembly in the early hours of 4 November. A resolution sponsored by the United States had passed the General Assembly on 2 November (64 to 5 with 6 abstentions) calling for a cease-fire, an end to military operations, the separation of the conflict from external actions, the withdrawal of forces to the 1949 armistice lines, and the reopening of the canal. It was an anti-Israeli step, and Israel agreed to a cease-fire on 3 November, on condition that Egypt also comply. Canada had abstained on that resolution because it did not propose U.N. police action and did not strike an adequate balance between Afro-Asian expectations and Anglo-French requirements. The Canadian resolution, adopted by the General Assembly on 4 November (57 to 0, with 19 abstentions), provided for the creation of a U.N. emergency force (UNEF) to supervise the cease-fire and to maintain order while the canal and Palestine questions were tackled. At Eisenhower's insistence, Anglo-French forces would not be allowed to participate in the UNEF. Pearson and Eisenhower (Dulles was now in the hospital for emergency surgery) hoped that the Anglo-French invasion force, lumbering toward Egypt, would turn back. It did not. Between 4 and 7 November, further General Assembly resolutions identified General E.L.M. Burns of Canada as the commander of the UNEF, reporting to the secretary-general, and confirmed that the UNEF would be independent, answerable only to the U.N. The General Assembly called on Britain, France, and Israel to honor the cease-fire and withdraw from Egyptian territory.

Eisenhower, initially very angry and feeling betrayed, asserted firm but judicious pressure on the aggressors to conform to the U.N. resolutions. He did not stand back from actual financial sanctions, threatened oil sanctions (three pumping stations on the pipelines from Iraq were blown up on 4 November and the canal was blocked), stern diplomatic representations including refusing to receive Eden, Lloyd, Mollet, or Ben-Gurion in Washington, and moral and personal pressure. He did not, however, support formal U.N. sanctions against the aggressors. He distanced himself from more extreme Afro-Asian positions and attempted to restore Western unity as promptly as it was wise and decent to do so. The British and French responded more promptly than the Israelis. Eisenhower was reelected in a landslide victory on 6 November.

There was always the possibility, in this final phase, that the Soviet Union, despite its concurrent actions to defeat the Hungarian revolt, would intervene at least diplomatically and attempt to find common cause with the United States in protecting Egypt and the U.N. Charter. The Soviet Union and the United States had cooperated in the Security Council on 30 and 31 October, although the United States had abstained on the Soviet resolution and the U.S.S.R. had voted for the U.S. resolution. In the first days of this final phase, the Soviet Union launched a propaganda attack on Israel and then on Britain and France, inside and beyond the U.N. It supported Egypt and called for appropriate measures to halt the aggression. The Soviet Union voted for the U.S. resolution in the General Assembly on 2 November but offered no military aid to Egypt. Soviet planes and crews were kept out of the battles against Israel. The Soviet Union also appealed to the nonaligned movement to act. Once the Hungarian situation was in hand, the Soviet Union increased its diplomatic and public pressure on Israel, Britain, and France. On 4 November, the Soviet Union held Britain and France responsible for the consequences of the crisis. On 5 November, Bulganin wrote to Eden, Mollet, and Ben-Gurion and published the content of the letters. He threatened them with nuclear attacks with "rocket equipment," and, if they did not withdraw from Egyptian territory within three days, he would call for U.N., specifically U.S. and Soviet, military assistance to Egypt. He proposed U.S.-U.S.S.R. joint military aid to Egypt directly to Eisenhower and activated the Security Council on 5 November to pursue that policy. A Soviet nuclear attack was highly improbable; Soviet military aid to Syria and Egypt was more possible and likely. The Soviet Union severed diplomatic relations with Israel on 5 November.

Eisenhower calculated soundly. He did not encourage these Soviet initiatives, which he judged self-serving, and acted independently using economic, diplomatic, personal, and moral pressures to end the military phase of the crisis. He did not cooperate with Bulganin against his European allies and Israel, and, indeed, he made clear his commitment to the unity of NATO and his determination to protect the joint interests of the West. He called the Soviet proposal for joint military action to end the Middle East crisis "preposterous." He stated, on 6 November, that only forces under the U.N. must enter the Middle East and that the United States would oppose unilateral intervention by any power. He called on the Soviet Union to evacuate its forces from Hungary. The problems that persisted after 7 November, particularly securing the withdrawal of Anglo-French and Israeli forces from Egyptian soil and establishing the UNEF, gave the Soviet Union ample opportunity to pose as the champions of peace and the Arabs. But such posturing merely increased Eisenhower's determination to craft a new, dynamic, and balanced Middle Eastern policy.

DISCUSSION QUESTIONS

1. *Which threats, and by whom, contributed to a negotiated settlement of this crisis?*
2. *What were the short-term risks and long-term costs of such threats?*
3. *What strategies worked best in this case and for whom? Which provided a foundation for subsequent policy toward the Middle East?*
4. *Did the U.S. role as spectator in the military action, as compared to one of direct participant in World War I, limit or expand its capacity to influence the subsequent peace negotiations? How did the multi-sided negotiating situation, involving conflicting interests of several parties, such as the United States, Egypt, Great Britain, France, Israel, the U.N., and the U.S.S.R., complicate or simplify the conditions for a settlement?*

FURTHER READING ON THE SUEZ

Beaufre, General Andre. *The Suez Expedition: 1956.* Translated by Richard Barry. London: Faber, 1969.

Bowie, Robert. *Suez 1956: International Crisis and the Rule of Law.* London: Oxford University Press, 1974.

Cooper, Chester L. *The Lion's Last Roar: Suez, 1956.* New York: Harper & Row, 1978.

Fawzi, Mahmoud. *Suez 1956: An Egyptian Perspective.* London: 1986).

Finer, Herman. *Dulles over Suez: The Theory and Practice of His Diplomacy.* Chicago: Quadrangle Books, 1964.

Lloyd, Selwyn. *The Suez 1956: A Personal Account.* London: Cape, 1978.

Thomas, Hugh. *The Suez Affair.* London: Harper & Row, 1967, 2d rev. ed., 1970.

Watt, Donald Cameron. *Documents on the Suez Crisis.* London: Royal Institute of International Affairs, 1957.

4

ENDING THE
VIETNAM WAR, 1972

The effort to negotiate a settlement of the Vietnam War was one of the longest, most frustrating, and controversial experiences in U.S. diplomacy. Between 1962, when the Kennedy administration secretly proposed negotiations to North Vietnam in Geneva, and 1972, when a breakthrough occurred in the secret talks in Paris between Henry Kissinger and Le Duc Tho, special negotiator for the North Vietnamese politburo, there were more than 2,000 documented efforts to bring Washington and Hanoi to the bargaining table. This case study focuses on the single successful effort to achieve negotiations over a draft agreement on ending the war and restoring peace in Vietnam.

The case begins by examining developments in the period from 8 to 22 October 1972, during which the North Vietnamese government (hereafter referred to as Hanoi or Democratic Republic of Vietnam [DRVN]) proposed an agreement for ending the war that, despite U.S. concurrence, was rejected by the South Vietnamese government (hereafter referred to as Saigon or Government of Vietnam [GVN]). This aspect of the case illustrates the difficulties of coordinating negotiating positions with allies who are not directly involved in the bargaining and whose goals are different. The focus then shifts to the U.S.-DRVN negotiations in November and December 1972, which attempt to resuscitate an agreement and illustrate the costs and benefits of using force to break a deadlock in negotiation.

This chapter is an edited version of the case study by Allan E. Goodman, The Vietnam Negotiations, October-December 1972, *Pew case study no. 307.*

REACHING THE DECISION TO NEGOTIATE

The story behind the breakthrough on 8 October 1972 in the secret negotiations between Washington and Hanoi, and especially the breakdown in those negotiations on 22 October, begins in midsummer of that year. By July, U.S. government officials had three indications that Hanoi might be prepared to negotiate an end to the war.

First, Hanoi's tone in the secret meetings between Henry Kissinger and Le Duc Tho changed from hostility to cordiality. Second, U.S. officials concluded from intelligence reports and captured Communist documents that Hanoi had begun to instruct its cadres in South Vietnam to prepare to compete politically with the government of Nguyen Van Thieu. Third, prisoner-of-war interrogation reports, moreover, indicated that the Communists' military leadership had planned a series of land-grabbing operations in the early fall to extend their apparent area of control in anticipation of a cease-fire-in-place. Consequently, Kissinger visited Saigon in late July to brief South Vietnamese president Nguyen Van Thieu on the secret talks. This was done partly to reassure Thieu that current press speculation predicting breakthroughs, which would involve either his ouster or U.S. support for a coalition government, was groundless. Technically, of course, this was correct. But Kissinger did not indicate to Thieu that because of the indications mentioned, he personally expected to reach an agreement with Hanoi.

In taking this step to brief Thieu, but only in general terms, Kissinger probably believed that trying to win Thieu's support before Hanoi was committed to a specific agreement would imperil the whole negotiating process. Kissinger feared that Thieu would leak details of the expected agreement, rally public opinion against it, and denounce Hanoi. He thought Thieu would be easier to persuade either if he were presented with a fait accompli and then given extensive military supplies before the agreement went into effect or if the North Vietnamese army (NVA) were dealt a military setback that assured there would be no offensive during the 1973 dry season. Kissinger doubted that Thieu would support the agreement without these conditions, even if the agreement were underpinned by understandings with Moscow and Peking that Hanoi would not be resupplied with the means to continue to wage conventional, large-unit warfare.

Kissinger and Tho met twice in August. For the first time in ten years of secret talks, the North Vietnamese negotiators were talking about a South Vietnam where a Communist and a non-Communist army and administration would have to coexist and Kissinger interpreted this rhetoric as a sign that Hanoi would not insist on Thieu's ouster. Shortly after the second meeting ended, Tho returned to Hanoi for consultations. Kissinger believed that the politburo would soon choose between war and peace. He again went to Saigon to meet with Thieu.

Unfortunately, Thieu believed Kissinger was wrong about Hanoi's willingness to negotiate a settlement of war. In a speech to the National Defense College in Saigon in August 1972, Thieu set out what he thought was ahead:

> There is only one way to force the Communists to negotiate seriously, and that consists of the total destruction of their economic and war potential. We must strike at them continuously, relentlessly, denying them any moment to catch their breath. . . . If our allies are determined, peace will be restored in Indochina. If they lack determination, the Communists will revert to their half-guerilla-half-conventional warfare, and the war will go on in Indochina forever."[1]

By 1972, the gap between Washington's and Saigon's expectations with respect to when, and on what terms, a negotiated settlement could be achieved was very wide. Kissinger sensed this during his discussions with Thieu, but he failed to adequately consider the possibility that when an agreement had been reached, Thieu would refuse to sign or that President Richard Nixon would permit Thieu to block a chance to have a negotiated settlement before the November election.

Another indication that Hanoi was ready to reach a negotiated settlement came on 11 September. On that day, the Communist Provisional Revolutionary Government of South Vietnam (hereafter referred to as the PRG) released what it described as an "important statement on ending . . . the war . . . and restoration of peace." The essence of that statement was the following proposal.

> If a correct solution is to be found to the Viet Nam problem, and a lasting peace ensured in Viet Nam, the U.S. government must meet the two following requirements:
>
> 1. To respect the Vietnamese people's right to true independence and the South Vietnamese people's right to effective self-determination: stop the U.S. war of aggression in Viet Nam; stop the bombing, mining, and blockade of the democratic republic of Viet Nam; completely cease the Vietnamization policy; terminate all U.S. military activities in South Viet Nam; rapidly and completely withdraw from South Viet Nam all U.S. troops, advisors, military personnel, technical personnel, weapons, and war materials and those of the other foreign countries in the U.S. camp; liquidate the

U.S. military bases in South Viet Nam; stop supporting the Nguyen Van Thieu stooge administration.

2. A solution to the internal problem of South Viet Nam must stem from the actual situation: there exist in South Viet Nam two administrations, two armies, and other political forces. It is necessary to achieve national concord: the parties of South Viet Nam must unite on the basis of equality, mutual respect, and mutual nonelimination; democratic freedoms must be guaranteed to the people. To this end, it is necessary to form in South Viet Nam a provisional government of national concord with three equal segments to take charge of the affairs of the period of transition and to organize truly free and democratic general elections.[2]

Kissinger detected in the PRG's proposal a willingness to settle for a cease-fire first, leaving the solution of internal political problems to subsequent negotiations between the GVN and the PRG. He also queried Soviet leader Leonid Brezhnev, himself fresh from talks with Le Duc Tho, and was assured that the PRG announcement signaled the beginning of real negotiations.

When Kissinger and Tho met on 15 September, Kissinger, therefore, made a personal plea for progress in the negotiations. As it stood, Kissinger said, the PRG proposal was not acceptable to President Nixon because it still implied that the United States and not the South Vietnamese people would remove Thieu from office. If the North Vietnamese could be more flexible on that point, Kissinger urged, they would find the president eager to reach a negotiated settlement than at that moment. But, he warned, after the election the president's position might very well harden, the prospects for negotiations dim, and the war continue.

At the next secret meeting (26 September 1972), Le Duc Tho proposed creating a tripartite National Council of Reconciliation and Concord (NCRC) that, though composed of the three equal segments, was not to be considered a government (something the PRG wanted); it would make decisions only on the principle of unanimity. Kissinger realized that this would be acceptable to President Nixon and thought it would be far more acceptable to Thieu than prior proposals that called for Thieu's resignation.[3]

Kissinger and Tho met again on 8 October. The meeting, however, began with very little sign that it would lead anywhere. To the U.S. participants in the meeting, Tho seemed suddenly truculent in tone and flatly stated that it was impossible to separate the military from a political settlement and demanded the resignation of Thieu as president of South Vietnam. However, just before the meeting was scheduled to conclude, Tho asked for a brief recess. When he returned, Tho handed Kissinger the English-language draft of an agreement. Initially it appeared to Kissinger as though Hanoi's draft could be the basis for at least an end to the fighting in South Vietnam, if not a political settlement of the war. The draft proposed an immediate cease-fire, U.S. troop withdrawal, and prisoner-of-war exchange. Each of these developments was to proceed according to a timetable that appeared independent of any progress made toward a political settlement. As Le Duc Tho described these and other features of the agreement in Vietnamese, however, U.S. language experts quickly realized that the terms used to describe the draft agreement in Vietnamese were ambiguous or objectionable and would certainly be opposed by the South Vietnamese government.

Kissinger viewed the draft as a significant breakthrough. As he later told the press, the North Vietnamese government

> dropped their demand for a coalition government which would absorb all existing authority. They dropped their demand for a veto over the personalities and the structure of the existing government. They agreed for the first time to a formula which permitted a simultaneous discussion of Laos and Cambodia. In short, we had for the first time a framework where, rather than exchange general propositions and measure our progress by whether dependent clauses of particular sentences had been minutely altered, we could examine concretely and precisely where we stood and what each side was prepared to give.[4]

Of particular concern to Kissinger's staff, in contrast, was a passage in the draft that called for the creation of an administration structure to achieve national reconciliation and concord, called in English the National Council of Reconciliation and Concord (NCRC). In Vietnamese the phrase "administrative structure" implied that such a body would have actual governmental authority. Thieu was certain to reject this portion of the draft.

Kissinger and Tho recessed their negotiations on 12 October so that Kissinger could take the draft to Washington for review. President Nixon then authorized Kissinger to pursue further negotiations. Kissinger returned to Paris on 17 October to tighten up the language and organize the agreement into a final, acceptable form. Le Duc Tho indicated that Hanoi wanted the agreement signed by the end of October and Kissinger promised he would do his utmost to meet this deadline.

Hanoi's Proposal of 8 October 1972

1. The United States respects the independence, sovereignty, unity and territorial integrity of Vietnam as recognized by the 1954 Geneva Agreements.
2. Twenty-four hours after the signing of the agreement, a cease-fire shall be observed throughout South Vietnam. The United States

will stop all its military activities and end the bombing and mining
in North Vietnam. Within 60 days there will be a total withdrawal
from South Vietnam of troops and military personnel of the United
States and those of the foreign countries allied with the United
States and with the Republic of Vietnam. The two South
Vietnamese parties shall not accept the introduction of troops,
military advisers and military personnel, armaments, munitions, and
war material into South Vietnam. The two South Vietnamese
parties shall be permitted to make periodical replacements of
armaments, munitions, and war material that have been worn out
or damaged after the cease-fire on the basis of piece for piece of
similar characteristics and properties. The United States will not
continue its military involvement or intervene in the internal affairs
of South Vietnam.

3. The return of all captured and detained personnel of the parties
shall be carried out simultaneously with the U.S. troops withdrawal.

4. The principles for the exercise of the South Vietnamese people's
right to self-determination are as follows: the South Vietnamese
people shall decide themselves the political future of South Vietnam
through genuinely free and democratic general elections under
international supervision, the United States is not committed to any
political tendency or to any personality in South Vietnam, and it
does not seek to impose a pro-American regime in Saigon: national
reconciliation and concord will be achieved, the democratic liberties
of the people ensured, an administrative structure called the
National Reconciliation and Concord of three equal segments will
be set up to promote the implementation of the signed agreements
by the Provisional Revolutionary Government of the Republic of
South Vietnam and the Government of the Republic of Vietnam
and to organize the general elections, the two South Vietnamese
parties will consult about the formation of councils at lower levels,
the question of Vietnamese armed forces in South Vietnam shall be
settled by the two South Vietnamese parties in a spirit of national
reconciliation and concord, equality and mutual respect, without
foreign interference, in accordance with the postwar situation,
among the questions to be discussed by the two South Vietnamese
parties are steps to reduce the military number on both sides and
to demobilize the troops being reduced, the two South Vietnamese
parties shall sign an agreement on the internal matters of South
Vietnam as soon as possible and will do their utmost to accomplish
this within three months after the cease-fire comes into effect.

5. The reunification of Vietnam shall be carried out step-by-step through peaceful means.
6. There will be formed a four-party joint military commission, and a joint military commission of the two South Vietnamese parties.

   An international commission of control and supervision shall be established.

   An international guarantee conference on Vietnam will be convened within 30 days of the signing of this agreement.
7. The government of the Democratic Republic of Vietnam, the Provisional Revolutionary Government of the Republic of South Vietnam, the government of the United States of America, and the government of the Republic of Vietnam shall strictly respect the Cambodian and Laos peoples' fundamental national rights as recognized by the 1954 Geneva Agreements on Indochina and the 1962 Geneva Agreements on Laos, i.e., the independence, sovereignty, unity and territorial integrity of these countries. They shall respect the neutrality of Cambodia and Laos. The government of the Democratic Republic of Vietnam, the Provisional Revolutionary Government of the Republic of South Vietnam, the government of the United States of America and the government of the Republic of Vietnam undertake to refrain from using the territory of Cambodia and the territory of Laos to encroach on the sovereignty and security of other countries. Foreign countries shall put an end to all military activities in Laos and Cambodia, totally withdraw from and refrain from introducing into these two countries troops, military advisers, and military personnel, armaments, munitions, and war material.

   The internal affairs of Cambodia and Laos shall be settled by the people of each of these countries without foreign interference.

   The problems existing between the three Indochinese countries shall be settled by the Indochinese parties on the basis of respect for each other's independence, sovereignty, and territorial integrity, and noninterference in each other's internal affairs.
8. The ending of the war, the restoration of peace in Vietnam will create conditions for establishing a new, equal, and mutually beneficial relationship between the Democratic Republic of Vietnam and the United States. The United States will contribute to healing the wounds of war and to postwar reconstruction in the Democratic Republic of Vietnam and throughout Indochina.
9. This agreement shall come into force as of its signing. It will be strictly implemented by all the parties concerned.

DISCUSSION QUESTIONS

1. *What assumption is Kissinger making about Hanoi's intentions and motivations? How should he respond to the concerns of and questions posed by his staff?*
2. *What strategy should he use to sell the agreement to the White House and to Saigon?*
3. *What are the costs, pitfalls, and benefits of working from Hanoi's draft?*

GETTING TO THE TABLE

Throughout this period, Thieu and his ambassador in Paris had been briefed only in the most general terms about the details of the secret talks. Thieu had not been informed of the breakthrough in early October, nor of the fact that an actual text had been prepared. Kissinger left Paris for Saigon on 17 October, confident that he could persuade Thieu to accept the agreement and that it could be initiated by 22 October, as Hanoi insisted.

Arriving in Saigon, Kissinger briefed U.S. ambassador Ellsworth Bunker, General Creighton Abrams (the commander of U.S. forces in Vietnam), and Bunker's deputy, Ambassador Charles Whitehouse.   As Kissinger later recounted,

> It was my first opportunity to show Bunker and his associates the current draft of the agreement. Bunker's reaction was that it exceeded what he had thought attainable; less would have been practically and morally justifiable. His opinion was shared by General Abrams; Abe reiterated what he had told Nixon, that there was no gain to be had in fighting another year on the present scale, adding that if we reduced our efforts by withdrawing the augmentation forces, conditions might well deteriorate. He reported the disquieting news that the North Vietnamese had launched a "high point" of offensive activities, especially around Saigon, obviously trying (as I was urging Saigon to try) to seize as much territory as possible before a cease-fire. Abrams thought this offensive would be troublesome, but also that it could be defeated without significant loss of territory.
>
> Charles Whitehouse was the only one present to raise a word of caution. He shared his colleagues' judgement of the agreement, but he doubted that Thieu would accept it before our election. For Saigon to cut the umbilical cord with the United States would be a wrenching psychological blow. Thieu would need many weeks to prepare himself

and his people for it. No matter what the terms, Thieu would prevaricate and delay as long as possible.[5]

Kissinger presented Thieu with an English draft of the agreement and a three-and-a-half-hour explanation of its importance on 19 October 1972. Kissinger wanted the South Vietnamese president to understand not only that the agreement made sense and protected Saigon's interests, but also that it would be difficult for the U.S. government to resist signing it. Therefore, Kissinger wrote that in his first meeting with Thieu,

> [Kissinger] began by outlining our strategy. Our Vietnam effort, I argued, had been held together by a very few people against massive domestic pressures seeking to liquidate our involvement in exchange for only the return of American prisoners. Those pressures would become uncontainable if we were perceived to abandon a reasonable negotiating position, especially when it was one we ourselves had put forward. I recognized that in this respect there was a difference between Thieu's imperatives and ours. He had to demonstrate to his people that he was firm; we had to demonstrate that we were flexible. I stressed that our concern was not the two weeks before our elections but the months that would follow. The additional costs of the military augmentation after the offensive, amounting already to $4.1 billion, would have to be submitted to the Congress in January. It would provide a convenient occasion for cutting off support. For over two years we had made a clearly defined set of proposals with Saigon's concurrence; these had been accepted by Hanoi. Even our supporters in the Congress would never understand if we now dragged our feet. That was the real deadline against which we were working. I spent an hour reviewing the entire draft, showing how in the cease-fire section it met every proposal we had put forward, and in its political provisions was far better than the terms we had offered publicly or privately.[6]

Thieu's response was noncommittal and cryptic. Aside from showing Kissinger and his delegation at the outset of their first meeting very little deference or courtesy, Thieu merely questioned some of the details of the draft, not Kissinger's interpretation and defense of it. Additional meetings with Thieu and his advisers were then scheduled. The next day, however, the Kissinger-Thieu discussions took a turn for the worse. Thieu and his advisers revealed that they did not agree with Kissinger's interpretation of the language of the agreement.

Linguistic problems and ambiguities indicated deeper and fundamental problems for Thieu's advisers. They had read between the lines of each provision in the draft to find evidence of Hanoi's perfidy, just as, it will be recalled, Kissinger's staff had done when they first read the Vietnamese version of the draft Le Duc Tho had prepared on 8 October. For example, Hanoi's draft called for the Vietnamese word for Paris to be the one that had come into vogue after the French defeat in 1954. In the provisions concerning troop withdrawal, the term for U.S. soldiers was actually slang meaning "dirty Yankee soldier." Within a day, Thieu's advisers had discovered some 129 linguistic changes that were "essential" before the documents could be signed by the GVN.

Saigon also had fundamental objections to the principle of cease-fire-in-place on which the agreement rested. Although Thieu had long suspected that Washington was willing to settle for such a cease-fire, he was no more inclined to accept it in 1972 than he had been in 1969, when his suspicion had first been aroused. Thieu saw the agreement as virtually guaranteeing that there would be continued warfare over the location of the front lines. Finally, Thieu argued that the provisions concerning inspection were weak. Of greatest concern was the absence of any reference to the status of the demilitarized zone and of any provision for an alternative means of obtaining a political settlement, should the two parties fail to reach an agreement within the prescribed ninety-day period for their negotiations.

In response, Kissinger questioned why Saigon was afraid—the GVN had the advantage of a million-man army that was well trained and well equipped. Thieu's reply was that South Vietnam was a nation of only 18 million people, and the costly maintenance of a large defense force would reduce the supply of potential development resources, resulting in his government's perpetual dependence on U.S. aid. Thieu was also deeply suspicious of the administrative structure to be set by the NCRC and labeled it a disguised coalition.

For the remainder of his visit, Kissinger tried a step-by-step approach in the negotiations with Thieu. He responded to each of the South Vietnamese objections to the agreement individually and made considerable progress in reducing the changes Saigon desired, from a list of more than one hundred down to a more manageable number of twenty-six. On the morning of 21 October, Kissinger met with the foreign minister of South Vietnam and his experts to go over the agreement and their proposed draft revisions. Over lunch with Ambassador Ellsworth Bunker, Kissinger described his and Bunker's outlooks as "quite optimistic"[7] as they awaited details on their next meeting with Thieu. Both expected that such a meeting would occur that afternoon. Ominously, there was no call from Thieu's aides to arrange such a meeting. Later that evening Kissinger and Bunker were informed that Thieu would see them the next morning at 8 A.M. Thieu also called Ambassador Bunker and emotionally accused the United States of attempting to plot a coup to overthrow him. Kissinger considered the call a bad omen for the meeting ahead and indicative of the frenzied, hostile atmosphere within Thieu's circle of advisers. But, as Kissinger observed,

> Nothing in Vietnam works as expected. The meeting with Thieu at 8:00 a.m. the next morning, Sunday, October 22, did not, after the ominous preliminaries, produce a confrontation. Indeed, it almost seemed as if Thieu had staged the melodrama of the previous day to establish a posture of independence that would make it possible for him to go along with us at the last moment. Thieu restated his by now familiar objections to the agreement. He focused on the continued presence of North Vietnamese troops and on the composition of the National Council, which had no functions, in which he was to have a veto, and which, as it turned out, never came into being. I answered Thieu's concerns point by point . . . Thieu responded with some dignity that for us the problem was how to end our participation in the war; for him it was a matter of life and death for his country. He had to consider not only the terms of the agreement but the perception of it by the people of South Vietnam. He was therefore consulting with the leaders of the National Assembly. He also wanted to hear a full report from his advisers on our reaction to the charges they proposed. He would meet Bunker and me again at 5:00 p.m. . . . . to give us his final reply. Bunker and I left the meeting encouraged. "I think we finally made a breakthrough," I optimistically cabled Washington.[8]

When this meeting was held, Thieu's reluctance to adhere to the provisions of the proposal was apparent. He justified his skepticism of Communist intentions by referring to an interview that had been held between North Vietnam's premier Pham Van Dong and Newsweek's senior editor Arnaud de Borchgrave on 18 October. Pham Van Dong began the interview with references to the failure of Vietnamization and the great victory that the DRVN's 1972 Easter military offensive symbolized; he described the United States from that point on as being forced to liquidate its commitments to Saigon. When asked if South Vietnamese president Thieu could participate in the process of political settlement that would follow the war, Pham replied, "Thieu has been overtaken by events." De Borchgrave asked what would happen after a cease-fire. Pham replied, "The situation will then be two armies and two administrations in the south, and given that situation, they will have to work out their own arrangements for a . . . coalition of transition."[9]

When the meeting with Thieu ended, Kissinger had to cable Washington that Thieu "rejected the entire plan or any modification of it and refuses to discuss any further negotiations on the basis of it."[10]

DISCUSSION QUESTIONS

1. *What could Kissinger have done to change Thieu's outlook on the situation and win his concurrence with the terms of the October draft agreement?*
2. *Should Kissinger have shared Thieu's concerns?*
3. *Could relations with the Thieu government have been handled with greater skill and sensitivity?*
4. *What were the sources of leverage available to the United States to force Thieu to accept the agreement and could they be fully used?*

FROM BREAKTHROUGH TO BREAKDOWN

On 24 October, South Vietnamese president Thieu publicly denounced the agreement as a ruse designed to provide the NVA with time to regroup its forces and to provide the Communists with a clear opportunity to gain political control of South Vietnam. Thieu believed they would do this by joining forces with his opponents, pressing with them for his ouster, and then subverting the police and army, which would leave the country extremely vulnerable to a new North Vietnamese military offensive. To avoid being placed in such a position, Thieu renewed his demand for the withdrawal of all NVA forces from South Vietnam and declared in a national radio address that in order to be prepared for a cease-fire, "the communist infrastructure must be wiped out quickly and mercilessly."[11]

Hanoi responded to Thieu's statements in a radio broadcast to its own the next day that excoriated him personally, blasted the Nixon administration for sabotaging a chance to end the war, and demanded that the Kissinger-Tho agreement be signed by 31 October. To Hanoi, concluding an agreement within a few days was essential. In the rush to claim insecure territory to enlarge the area of Communist control with a cease-fire in place, many PRG military units revealed themselves prematurely and were now the targets of GVN police and army attacks. The North Vietnamese also feared that Washington would try to strengthen Saigon's war-fighting capability significantly if protracted negotiations ensued.

At this point, resorting to public diplomacy, Kissinger called a press conference for 26 October (his first on national television) the purpose of which "was to rescue from Vietnamese hatreds a fragile agreement that would end a decade of agony." The press conference was designed to "reassure Hanoi that we would stand by the basic agreement," leave open "the possibility of raising Saigon's suggested changes," and "convey to Saigon that we were determined to proceed on course."[12] Kissinger expected that further negotiations with both Hanoi and Saigon would be required to complete the agreement. But, as he told the press, "What stands in the way of an agreement now are issues that are relatively less important than those that have already been settled." It was in this context that Kissinger made his ill-fated statement "Peace is at hand."

But Hanoi did not respond to Washington's requests to resume negotiations until 4 November. The date the North Vietnamese proposed was 14 November. On 7 November, Kissinger replied by proposing 15 November (to enable his assistant, General Alexander Haig, to travel to Saigon in an effort this time to assure Thieu's concurrence with the U.S. negotiating approach). Hanoi replied to this proposal on 8 November and postponed the date further, suggesting 20 November and indicating that Le Duc Tho was currently ill. On 9 November the United States agreed to a meeting on the 20th.

When the Kissinger-Tho negotiations resumed in Paris, they did so in an atmosphere of hostility and mistrust, resulting, according to Kissinger, in a series of "sterile exchanges"[13] over the specific issues summarized in the accompanying chart (see page 76). Le Duc Tho appeared wary of Kissinger and his authority, apparently thinking Kissinger had negotiated an agreement in October that exceeded his instructions and failed to persuade Nixon and Thieu to accept it. The U.S. side was increasingly alarmed, moreover, about apparent Communist plans to use the first few days and weeks of postagreement confusion as a screen for attacks against the GVN. And from the start, Kissinger was particularly worried about his lack of leverage on Hanoi in the face of a likely congressional cutoff of further funds for the war.

In the meetings with Hanoi that followed, Kissinger represented both Washington and Saigon. He put forward some sixty-nine linguistic and other changes in the agreement demanded by President Thieu but largely "to avoid the charge that we were less than meticulous in guarding Saigon's concerns" because Thieu had been warned "there was no possibility of obtaining this many changes." In retrospect, Kissinger considers the putting forward of all of Thieu's demands "a major tactical mistake" because "it must have strengthened Hanoi's already strong temptation to dig in its heels and push me against our Congressional deadlines."[14]

The other set of issues Kissinger introduced represented the minimum demands of the United States: Unless they were satisfied, Kissinger told Tho, an agreement could not be signed. These demands centered on the problems likely to occur in the first few weeks and months that the agreement was in force, problems raised by expected military operations aimed at extending Communist territorial control. It was essential to Kissinger, for example, that the cease-fire supervisory mechanism be in place and able to function effectively when the agreement was signed. Equally essential was the clarification of the military status of the demilitarized zone (DMZ), an issue that Thieu wanted raised because it directly affected the sovereignty of the GVN. Kissinger's approach was to downplay the sovereignty aspect of this issue and to discuss the DMZ in terms of its role in assuring that there would be a cease-fire. Consistent with its objective of retaining an unimpaired capability to resume the military struggle if the political evolution specified in the agreement did not occur, Hanoi had sought only the vaguest of characterizations of the DMZ.

Kissinger's strategy for dealing with all of the linguistic problems posed by the agreement's translation into Vietnamese was to delete as many of the ambiguous or objectionable phrases as possible. Issues of principle that could not be included in the actual text of the agreement because Hanoi flatly refused to commit itself publicly to them were left to a series of under-standings that became part of the official, classified record.

The basic tightening up of the agreement sought by Washington did not come easily. As Kissinger was methodically working through the U.S. agenda, the North Vietnamese were introducing new demands as the implied price for making the changes Washington sought. In the November meetings, for example, Hanoi reintroduced demands for the removal of Thieu as South Vietnam's president, the simultaneous release of political prisoners with the prisoners of war (POWs) and a significant strengthening rather than diminution of the powers of the National Council of Reconciliation and Concord, the body on which the Communist PRG would have equal voice with the GVN over future political evolution in South Vietnam. Frequently, also, Hanoi would negotiate by dropping its insistence on the wording of a particular article of the agreement, only to have the objectionable wording appear in its version of the aforementioned "understandings."

One of the U.S. negotiators recalled that

> by the middle of our November meetings, there was clearly an attitude of dalliance on Hanoi's part, and it was then that Nixon told us to begin warning Hanoi in no uncertain terms that a failure to negotiate seriously would result in a renewal of the bombing. Serious negotiations from our perspective meant that Hanoi should cooperate in clarifying the linguistic ambiguities, working out the protocols, and staying within the framework of the October draft.[15]

Such warnings and expectations were conveyed to Le Duc Tho in a ninety-minute meeting on 24 November. At that meeting, Kissinger also pointedly warned Hanoi that thereafter the bombing, suspended in October, based on the president's prediction that an agreement was near, could be easily resumed, and with a much greater intensity.

The next round of the negotiations lasted from 4 to 14 December. From the start of this round, it was clear to Kissinger that Hanoi, in the person of Le Duc Tho, was unwilling to do more than posture and accuse the U.S. government of bad faith. Nevertheless, Kissinger still hoped that all remaining issues could be settled by diplomacy and proposed to Tho a specific scenario that would lead to signing an agreement before Christmas.

However, as Kissinger reported to President Nixon in a cable after the first day of meetings, Le Duc Tho

> rejected every change we asked for, asked for a change on civilian prisoners requiring all those alleged to be held by Saigon to be released simultaneously with the release of military POW's, demanded the withdrawal of American civilians from South Vietnam thus making the maintenance of the Vietnam air force impossible, and withdrew some concessions from last week. In short, we would wind up with an agreement significantly worse than what we started with. I told him flatly that his approach did not provide the basis for a settlement. In the ensuing dialogue Tho stuck firmly by his intransigent position. The only alternative he offered to his presentation this afternoon was to go back to the October agreement literally with no changes by either side.[16]

Late in the evening of 5 December, after Kissinger and his staff had "spent hours . . . seeking to distill some ray of hope" from what Le Duc Tho had said, Kissinger concluded "that the only hope of averting a collapse would be messages to Moscow and Peking."[17] These messages contained Kissinger's appraisal that the resumed talks were leading nowhere, that a "breakup" was "probable," and that the United States would have to react militarily to avert or break a deadlock. The Chinese never responded to Kissinger's message. Moscow "counseled patience, expressed confidence in Hanoi's desire for peace, and assured us . . . that the North Vietnamese were still ready to sign an agreement within the October framework."[18] Nevertheless, when the talks resumed on 6 and 7 December, Kissinger found only "continued procrastination" on the part of Hanoi.[19] There also ensued a series of telegraphic exchanges between Nixon and Kissinger that convinced the president that there was "no way of sustaining an effective negotiations strategy" through the administration's public diplomacy. "Only fear of resumed military operations would keep Hanoi on course."[20]

Kissinger and Tho met again on 6 December. According to Kissinger,

> Both sides reviewed their positions. There was some tinkering with individual clauses, but we were simply treading water. The best proof

of Hanoi's reluctance to settle was Le Duc Tho's continuing refusal to permit a meeting of the experts to negotiate the detailed protocols even on provisions not in dispute, Le Duc Tho said they were "studying our documents" and theirs were not ready. Hence, no matter what he and I decided, it could not be implemented until the experts had concluded a task the North Vietnamese refused to begin.[21]

Another meeting was held the next day, at which point Kissinger concluded that to Hanoi, "the lapse of time could only improve its position." Thus, to Kissinger "December 7 marked the beginning of the real deadlock."[22]

Over the next seven days, Hanoi managed to keep an agreement in view but effectively out of reach. On 8 December, Tho allowed what Kissinger termed "major steps forward" with respect to the authority of the NCRC (it was no longer to be called even an "administrative" structure because that phrase still translated into Vietnamese in a way that suggested the council would have actual government authority) and the separation of the issue of freeing civilian and military POWs, but he made unacceptable demands with respect to the status of the DMZ and essentially prohibited U.S. technicians from helping South Vietnam to maintain its air force. This latter issue was conceded by Tho the next day but he insisted that military movement through the DMZ be permitted. When Kissinger proposed a compromise that would permit civilians and nonmilitary officials to move across the DMZ, Tho, apparently taken aback, "suddenly complained of a headache, high blood pressure, general debility,"[23] which required what amounted to a forty-eight-hour recess until 11 December.

When Kissinger and Tho met again, Tho scuttled other parts of the agreement.

> First he rejected signing procedures that we had assumed settled. (This was a complex arrangement by which Saigon could sign without recognizing the Communist Provisional Revolutionary Government.) Next, forty-eight hours after conceding the issue of American civilian technicians assisting South Vietnamese armed forces, he insisted that his applied only to the public text of the agreement to avoid embarrassing us. He now asked for a written private understanding that our technicians would be withdrawn. He also, regretfully, was not yet ready to discuss any of the protocols. And his instructions on the DMZ would not arrive until next day. Le Duc Tho, in short, made it clear that he would not settle that day, nor (given the outstanding issues) was a settlement likely on the morrow.[24]

On 12 December, Tho indicated that he had at last received instructions from Hanoi on the status of the DMZ.

> He had a proposal that omitted the phrase "civilian" from any formula for permitted movement across the DMZ. In other words, Hanoi wanted to leave open the right of military transit through a Demilitarized Zone, one of the neater tricks of diplomacy, and one that raised even further doubts about the ban on infiltration. To ease our pain, Tho finally produced protocols for the cease-fire and international control machinery. He now preempted our plans by informing me that he had decided to leave Paris for Hanoi on Thursday, December 14, taking four or five days to get there. He would not be able to settle unless he could personally convert the recalcitrants in the Politburo who were constantly giving him a hard time, especially on the DMZ. He offered to return if necessary, but thought we could settle the remaining issues by an exchange of messages, a patent absurdity given the many technical details still requiring attention. The idea of a pacific Tho constrained by his bellicose peers from making concessions was mind-boggling; but it served Tho's purpose of stalling without (he hoped) giving an excuse to retaliate.[25]

At this point, Kissinger cabled Nixon,

> I have come to the following conclusions. Hanoi has decided to play for time, either because of the public split between us and Saigon; or because they have a pipeline into South Vietnam and know about our exchanges; or because their leadership is divided and they are still making up their minds on whether to conclude the agreement. Their consistent pattern is to give us just enough each day to keep us going but nothing decisive which could conclude an agreement. On the other hand, they wish to insure that we have no solid pretext for taking tough actions. They keep matters low-key to prevent a resumption of bombing. They could have settled in three hours any time these past few days if they wanted to, but they have deliberately avoided this. . . .
> They have reduced the issues to a point where a settlement can be reached with one exchange of telegrams. I do not think they will send this telegram, however, in the absence of strong pressures.[26]

Kissinger, in fact, believed that each day of his latest round of negotiations brought the United States and Hanoi "further away from an agreement."[27]

In his final cable from Paris, Kissinger thus argued:

We now have two essential strategic choices. The first one is to turn hard on Hanoi and increase pressure enormously through bombing and other means. This would include measures like reseeding the mines, massive two-day strikes against the power plants over this weekend, and a couple of B-52 efforts. This would make clear that they paid something for these past ten days. Concurrently . . . pressures on Saigon would be essential so that Thieu does not think he has faced us down, and we can demonstrate that we will not put up with our ally's intransigence any more than we will do so with our enemy.

The second course is to maintain present appearances by scheduling another meeting with Le Duc Tho in early January. This would test the extremely unlikely hypothesis that Tho might get new instructions. If we were once again stonewalled, we would then turn hard on Hanoi. We would give up the current effort, blaming both Vietnamese parties but placing the major onus on Hanoi. We would offer a bilateral deal of withdrawal and an end of bombing for prisoners.[28]

Back in Washington, and deeply pessimistic about prospects for further productive negotiations, Kissinger and Nixon feared that Hanoi would now revert to the tactics of stalling for time in the expectation that U.S. domestic pressures and the rift between Washington and Saigon would force acceptance of an agreement that would give Communist Provisional Revolutionary Government (PRG) actual political authority and would allow the North Vietnamese army to operate with impunity in South Vietnam. Thus, as Kissinger wrote in his memoirs, when

Nixon, Haig and I met on the morning of December 14 to consider our course . . . we were agreed that if we did nothing we would wind up paralyzed. . . . There was no reason to expect Hanoi to change its tactics if talks did resume in January . . . we had only two choices: Taking a massive, shocking step to impose our will on events and end the war quickly, or letting matters drift into another round of inconclusive negotiations, prolonged warfare, bitter national divisions, and mounting casualties. There were no other options."[29]

DISCUSSION QUESTIONS

1. *Was Kissinger's assessment of Hanoi's intentions correct?*
2. *What would you have done at this point through diplomacy and bargaining to change Hanoi's outlook on the situation and its attitude toward the negotiations and the October draft agreement?*

3. *Was it reasonable to turn, as Kissinger did in December, to Moscow and Peking and expect them to press Hanoi to negotiate in earnest?*

4. *Should Kissinger have had more patience?*

5. *And did he have more options than those he presented at the 14 December meeting in the White House?*

6. *How would you assess the coordination of military actions and diplomatic overtures? At this point, to what degree did domestic U.S. politics impose constraints on the American negotiators and reduce their bargaining power?*

7. *How did the U.S. role as a primary negotiator in the peace talks and direct participant in the military action serve to influence the course of the negotiations? What were the constraints? How did the U.S. negotiating role in the Vietnam talks differ from their position in the World War II talks?*

Table 1   Central Issues in the Vietnam Negotiations
              November-December 1972[30]

Central Issues	DRVN/PRG Position	U.S./GVN Position
Civilian Political Prisoners	Release of civilian political prisoners should be linked to releasing POWs	Release of civilian political prisoners independent of U.S. POWs
American Civilian Technicians	Technicians should be withdrawn along with U.S. troops	Technicians should be allowed to stay
National Council of Reconciliation and Concord	Should be called an "administrative structure" in the agreement and imply actual government authority	Should simply be called the NCRC and imply no such authority
Status of the Demilitarized Zone	Legal status of DMZ to be discussed after agreement signed	Both sides should be obligated to respect DMZ as demarcation line between North and South Vietnam; military movement across it prohibited
NVA in the South	The NVA should be allowed to remain as part of a cease-fire in place	The new units that came south to participate in the Easter Offensive should be withdrawn; other NVA units can remain
Cease-fire in Laos	To follow 30 days after an agreement	Should allow an agreement within a week to 10 days
Machinery of the International Commission on Control and Supervision (ICCS)	Can only investigate a report with unanimous approval of members; no independent logistical capability	Should be strengthened and in place at the time agreement goes into effect
Resupply of weapons to the GVN	Only "worn out or damaged" weapons could be replaced	"Destroyed" or "used up" weapons could be replaced
Signing Procedures	All parties should sign agreement and be named in it	Two virtually identical agreements to be signed: one between the U.S. and the DRVN on behalf of the GVN and PRG and another that referred only to "the parties participating in the Paris Conference," which U.S. and GVN would sign on one page and the DRVN and PRG on another

NOTES

1. Translated in Allan E. Goodman's *The Lost Peace: America's Search for a Negotiated Settlement of the Vietnam War* (Stanford, CA: Hoover Institution Press, 1978), p. 126.

2. *Ibid.*, p. 127.

3. Prophetically, however, only three days later in a speech to Saigon University students, Thieu declared, "If the United States accepts to withdraw its troops unconditionally, the Communists will win militarily. If we accept a coalition, we will lose politically." *Ibid.*, p. 129. Throughout the summer and fall of 1973 Thieu never wavered in his conviction that, despite whatever the North Vietnamese called the organization to be created as part of a political settlement, it was a disguised coalition.

4. Henry Kissinger, press conference, 26 October 1972.

5. Henry Kissinger, *White House Years* (Boston: Little, Brown & Co., 1979), p. 1367.

6. *Ibid.*, pp. 1369-1370.

7. *Ibid.*, p. 1379.

8. *Ibid.*, p. 1382.

9. "Exclusive From Hanoi," *Newsweek*, 30 October 1972, p. 26.

10. *Ibid.*, p. 1385.

11. Goodman, *The Lost Peace*, p. 138.

12. Kissinger, *White House Years*, p. 1398.

13. *Ibid.*, p. 1427.

14. *Ibid.*

15. Goodman, *The Lost Peace*, p. 158.

16. Kissinger, *White House Years*, p. 1429.

17. *Ibid.*, pp. 1429-1430.

18. *Ibid.*, p. 1432.

19. *Ibid.*, p. 1434.

20. *Ibid.*, p. 1431.

21. *Ibid.*, p. 1432.

22. *Ibid.*, p. 1434.

23. *Ibid.*, p. 1437.

24. *Ibid.*, p. 1439.

25. *Ibid.*, p. 1441.

26. *Ibid.*, p. 1442.

27. *Ibid.*, p. 1444.

28. *Ibid.*, pp. 1444-1445.

29. *Ibid.*, pp. 1447-1448.

30. Goodman, *The Lost Peace*, pp. 186-187.

FURTHER READING ON VIETNAM

Duncanson, Dennis J. *Government and Revolution in Vietnam*. London: Oxford University Press, 1968.

Herz, Martin F. *The Vietnam War in Retrospect*. Washington, DC: School of Foreign Service, Georgetown University, 1968.

Karnow, Stanley. *Vietnam: A History*. New York: Penguin Books, 1984.

Kolko, Gabriel. *Anatomy of a War: Vietnam, the United States and the Modern Historical Experience*. New York: Pantheon Books, 1985.

Nixon, Richard M. *No More Vietnams*. New York: Arbor House, 1985.

Turley, William S. *The Second Indochina War: A Short Political and Military History*. Boulder, CO: Westview Press, 1986.

5

MEDIATION DURING
THE WAR IN THE
FALKLANDS/MALVINAS, 1982

The world awoke on 2 April 1982 to the news that the Argentine army and navy had invaded and occupied the Falkland Islands, a tiny British dependency in the South Atlantic with 1,800 inhabitants.

In Buenos Aires there was rejoicing, as Argentinians celebrated the recovery of the islands, long claimed by Argentina under the name Islas Malvinas. In London there was shock and outrage; people who had not even heard of the islands before the invasion demanded action to regain them. The government was deeply embarrassed; the foreign secretary, Lord Peter Carrington, resigned, and there were calls for Prime Minister Margaret Thatcher's resignation as well. In the House of Commons, the British government pledged itself to recover the islands by any means necessary, including force.

In Washington, the U.S. government reacted with dismay and grave concern. A volatile conflict between two highly valued U.S. allies clearly posed great risks for U.S. policy. Balanced on one side was the special relationship with Great Britain, one of the oldest allies of the United States and a major NATO (North Atlantic Treaty Organization) country, and on the other side was friendly relations with the Argentine government, considered the U.S.'s most reliable friend in Latin America. Support for either disputant would risk damaging U.S. ties with the other ally, possibly irreparably. The focus of this case is on the effort to prevent and then end the war by mediation.

This chapter is an edited version of the case study by Chaim D. Kaufmann, U.S. Mediation in the Falklands/Malvinas Crisis: Shuttle Diplomacy in the 1980s, *Pew case study no. 431.*

REACHING THE DECISION TO NEGOTIATE

Although the invasion was unexpected, the dispute over control of the islands dated back to the period of 1833 British occupation. Argentina claimed that the islands, originally a Spanish possession, were inherited by Argentina upon achieving independence. In support of their own position, the British refuted the earlier Spanish claims to the islands and also invoked the principle of self-determination. For its part, the United States had never officially supported either claim.

In 1965, U.N. General Assembly Resolution 2065 directed Argentina and Great Britain to negotiate the sovereignty of the islands. Although discussions continued until 1982, they were unproductive because of the irreconcilable positions of the two parties. Argentina would not settle for less than sole sovereignty, whereas Britain was held hostage by the pro-British inclinations of the residents. Meanwhile, the Argentinians grew more impatient, as a military junta secured control in 1976 and recognized the need for a foreign policy success as a diversion from domestic failures.

From a U.S. perspective, the Reagan administration initiated a new policy toward the Western Hemisphere in 1981. The "Reagan Doctrine" committed the United States to the unqualified support of all friendly, anticommunist regimes in the hemisphere, whether democratic or authoritarian. Consequently, criticism of Argentine human rights violations was relaxed and relations improved. Argentina supported U.S. policy in Central America and emerged as the most valuable friend of the United States in the hemisphere.

In March 1982, British intelligence officials concluded that an Argentinian action against the Falklands was likely and the foreign secretary formally requested U.S. diplomatic help on 28 March. In response, Secretary of State Alexander Haig and President Ronald Reagan warned the Argentine junta that an invasion would seriously damage U.S.-Argentine relations.

Following the invasion, Britain severed diplomatic relations with Argentina, froze Argentine assets, and prepared a naval task force to retake the islands. Britain also asked the United States, the EEC, and Britain's Commonwealth partners to impose sanctions on Argentina. The EEC and Commonwealth countries responded promptly. In addition, Britain sponsored a successful resolution in the U.N. calling for both an immediate cessation of hostilities and an immediate Argentine withdrawal from the islands (Resolution 502).

Under these circumstances, the invasion presented the U.S. government with a foreign policy crisis for which it was almost totally unprepared. The crisis was brought to a head almost immediately when Britain requested U.S. military assistance on a variety of issues, beginning with permission to use Wideawake Air Force Base on Ascension Island, in the South Atlantic about 3,000 miles from the Falklands.[1] They also requested access to satellite intelligence and help with certain critical supplies, such as aviation fuel.[2] The British had to be given an answer, and a general U.S. policy toward the Falklands crisis had to be formulated without delay.

President Reagan did not take an active leadership role, leaving the main tasks primarily to the State Department. However, the department's top policymakers who confronted the issue in the first few days of April, were divided along both ideological and bureaucratic lines into two distinct camps: a pro-British group led by Secretary Haig and Lawrence Eagleburger (then undersecretary of state for political affairs but previously the assistant secretary for European affairs) and a pro-Argentine group headed by U.N. ambassador Jeanne Kirkpatrick and Thomas Enders (assistant secretary of state for Latin American affairs). Of top decisionmakers outside the State Department, Defense Secretary Caspar Weinberger and Deputy Director of Central Intelligence Bobby Inman were generally pro-British, whereas National Security Adviser Judge William Clark tended to support Argentina.

The two sides in this debate could not agree on policy because they were not in accord about the relative importance of the U.S. interests at stake. For instance, the "Latin Americanist" group focused on the anticolonial justice of Argentine claims and the importance, and fragility, of U.S. relations with Latin America. Enders predicted that U.S. support for Britain would endanger the carefully rebuilt ties with Latin American states, reducing hopes for gaining their aid in combating Soviet and Cuban influence in the hemisphere. Putting it even more strongly, Kirkpatrick warned that supporting Britain would earn the United States "a hundred years of animosity in Latin America."[3]

This group advocated treating the sovereignty issue on its merits: Argentina had the better claim, which the United States should respect. The junta's resort to force, though regrettable, had to be considered an understandable response to frustration at Britain's delay and lack of good faith in the sovereignty negotiations ever since 1965. The night before the invasion, in fact, Kirkpatrick and Enders had attended a dinner given by Argentina's ambassador in Washington, and during the evening Kirkpatrick predicted that, based on the traditional pattern of neutrality regarding the sovereignty issue, the United States would not view the invasion as aggression.[4] Reportedly, Ambassador Kirkpatrick believed that "the Argentinians have been claiming for 200 years that they own those islands. If they own those islands, then moving troops into them is not armed aggression."[5]

However, for Haig and the pragmatists the significant issues were determined to be Argentina's unprovoked aggression and the U.S.'s loyalty to its special relationship with Britain. To this group it was obvious that Britain was the more important of the two allies, not only historically but also based on the recent support and services that the Thatcher government had provided the United States on contentious NATO issues, such as the deadlocked Intermediate-range Nuclear Forces (INF) negotiations, the deployment of cruise missiles in Europe, and the attempts to block construction of the Soviet natural-gas pipeline. The U.S. reputation as a reliable ally was also at stake. As Haig put it, to fail in this test would reveal the United States as a "fair-weather ally," with uncertain but probably serious effects not only on British policy but on the cohesion of the whole Western alliance system.

Neither Britain nor the United States could acquiesce in Argentina's use of force. In Haig's mind, the junta's action was analogous to Hitler's because they both saw the West as too weak and decadent to resist, and if they succeeded, others would be emboldened to do likewise. The precedent would be especially dangerous for Latin America, where numerous border disputes remain unresolved, including those between Peru and Ecuador, Guatemala and Belize, Venezuela and Guyana, and Argentina and Chile. As Haig saw it, "The whole of the West was engaged in the crisis on both moral and practical planes."[6] The group's bottom line, therefore, was that Argentina not be rewarded for its aggression. Any solution must begin with Argentine withdrawal; only then could sovereignty questions be discussed.

Eagleburger advocated an immediate commitment of help to Britain on all levels. Haig, however, though agreeing with his deputy on most of the issues involved, was responsible as secretary of state for integrating the policy of the entire U.S. government. His first priority was to attempt to achieve a peaceful resolution, which might allow the United States to avoid a public tilt toward Britain and alienation of the Latin Americans, and to prevent a war, which would probably open the way for increased Soviet influence not only in Argentina but throughout the Spanish-speaking hemisphere.[7] Eagleburger, however, had an experience early in the crisis that convinced him that the problem had been overstated.

> [A certain Latin American leader] came to see me, and he had a number of his entourage with him, and I got the ritual lecture on American support for colonialism, the British, the Falklands, and so forth, in front of his group. And then as they got up to leave, he stayed behind, and as the rest of them left he closed the door, and he said: "Don't you let those admirals and generals win in the Falklands; we have our own admirals and generals, and I don't want them to get the wrong ideas."[8]

Diverging slightly from Haig and Eagleburger, Admiral Inman advocated at least limited support of Britain, although based on a somewhat different rationale. Primarily he was concerned that failure to support Britain would endanger long-standing Anglo-American intelligence cooperation in a number of areas around the globe. He reported: "I took the very strong view that [use of Ascension] was within their legal rights, and that there were many places in the world, where we in fact occupied facilities, Diego Garcia, Hong Kong, Bermuda, where the British had not denied us the ability to use facilities for whatever we did."[9]

In any case, the Organization of American States (OAS) was scheduled to take up the issue within a few days and Argentina was expected to receive the support of virtually every other member. If the United States held out, it would be isolated in the embarrassing position of breaking hemispheric solidarity. Argentina could also be expected to try to invoke the Rio Pact of 1947, the hemispheric defense treaty. Nevertheless, this prospect posed a lesser dilemma, because defining the aggressor would be problematic and Argentina would be unlikely to seek direct military help in that forum.[10]

At first, U.S. officials could not even agree on the reality of the crisis; the pro-British faction believed that the crisis would lead to war if not resolved quickly, whereas the pro-Argentine group saw the British counterinvasion threat as a bluff and believed that the British would soon resign themselves to the situation if diplomatic efforts made little headway.[11] Both factions' beliefs on this issue were driven in turn by their assessments of the likely outcome of a military contest. The Latin Americanists argued that reconquest would be impossible without massive U.S. help. Most of the other decision-makers expected that the British could probably succeed, but at great expense and with high risk. Only Haig seems to have been certain from the start that the British would win.

The policymakers also had to consider the impact of U.S. public opinion, which strongly favored Great Britain. To most in the United States, aiding Britain when it was attacked was only a natural reaction, and few knew or cared much about the delicate interactions between U.S.-Argentine relations and the civil wars in El Salvador and Nicaragua, let alone the rights and wrongs of who owned the Falklands. Speaking to Nicholas Henderson, the British ambassador to Washington, one U.S. senator explained very simply, "Why I am with you? It's because you are British."[12]

DISCUSSION QUESTIONS

1. *Haig and the other officials had to choose among three basic options for U.S. policy: a relatively passive neutral stance, open support for Britain, or active U.S. diplomatic efforts to try to mediate a solution. How realistic was it to expect that Britain and Argentina could settle the dispute peacefully themselves?*
2. *Could the U.S. government maintain a neutral stance during this period?*
3. *Which side was able to use the passing of time to its advantage?*

4. *Could the United States use its influence with both parties to attempt to mediate a peaceful solution?*

5. *Preliminary discussion with both sides revealed willingness to consider U.S. mediation. This option appeared to offer the best chance of avoiding war, but depending on the line the United States would take in negotiations also ran the risk of offending both sides. Who would make the most effective mediator for the U.S. government? For the OAS? For the U.N.?*

GETTING TO THE TABLE

No real consensus was reached in the series of State Department and National Security Council (NSC) meetings held on 5, 6, and 7 April, with the result that U.S. policy was determined mainly by Haig and Eagleburger, the responsible State Department officers, although this did not prevent Enders and Kirkpatrick from continuing to bring their own views to separate conversations with the president and National Security Adviser Clark. On the evening of the 6th, Haig recommended to Reagan that the United States offer to mediate, and he offered to head the mediation team personally. The president agreed.

The key members of the mediation team were Haig, Enders, David Gompert (deputy undersecretary for political affairs, Eagleburger's deputy), and General Vernon Walters (President Reagan's special "roving ambassador" and a personal friend of Argentine president General Leopoldo Galtieri).

Everyone recognized that reconciling the parties would be a difficult endeavor, and Haig realized that failure might enable his enemies to force his resignation. As he said to his wife, "If the situation cannot be saved, and this is very possible, then whatever I do will be seen as failure, even if it is a success in larger terms than the conflict itself. I'm going because I have to, but it may turn out to be my Waterloo."[13]

The mediation was undertaken "shuttlestyle." The team went first to London on the 8th, then to Buenos Aires on the 9th, to London again on the 12th, then to Washington, and back to Buenos Aires again by the 17th. The initial positions of the two sides could hardly have been further apart. Thatcher demanded that Argentina fulfill the requirements of Resolution 502 and withdraw completely before sovereignty be discussed. The Argentinians were willing to discuss a temporary withdrawal, but only on the condition that the withdrawal be preceded by an agreement to resolve the sovereignty issue in Argentina's favor by the end of 1982. Both sides were willing to envision some kind of interim administration for the islands, possibly involving U.S. or U.N. participation, although the British required that such a government be "recognizably British" whereas the Argentinians insisted on equal participation. However, the real sticking point was sovereignty. The British absolutely refused to concede the issue before negotiations and the Argentines would not withdraw without guarantees.[14]

In fact, neither government had much room for maneuver, as the invasion had kindled intense patriotic feeling in both Argentina and Britain. The British government, under heavy criticism for failing to foresee the invasion, had silenced its opponents by wrapping itself in the flag and promising to recover the islands no matter what. For their part, the Argentine junta had converted public discontent to enthusiastic support by seizing the islands. After focusing public attention on the Argentine invasion and then exploiting this foreign policy triumph to suppress domestic protests, the junta members could foresee the backlash that would follow retreat. As Gompert put it, "Any political solution that would permit the survival of one government would likely bring down the other."[15]

In addition, even after the battle force was already on its way, the Argentine leaders, especially the navy, did not believe Britain would fight. The U.S. mediators came away from London firmly convinced of British resolve, but the junta members would not credit this. To them, a colonial war in 1982 was an absurd and hopeless enterprise. As Galtieri told Haig, "If the British wish to send another army, we will receive this anachronistic colonialist expedition with appropriate honors."[16] The Argentinians also tried to put pressure on the U.S. mediators by organizing public demonstrations of support for their Malvinas occupation and by privately threatening to seek military help from the Soviets if necessary. Galtieri even told Haig that the Soviets had offered to sink the carrier HMS *Invincible* by submarine and let Argentina take credit; Haig considered that totally incredible but did take seriously the likelihood of increased Soviet influence if the Argentinians lost trust in the United States.[17]

On the tactical level, the mediators would have to determine the new balance that they would strike between the two sides. Haig's view was that to maintain an "honest broker" status during negotiations would require holding off on aid to Britain. Conversely, until an agreement was actually reached, the United States could not pressure the British to delay their military plans. This in turn meant that any mediation effort would have to succeed in less time than it would take the British fleet to reach the Falklands, about three weeks at the most.

Haig and Enders, although not Eagleburger, also saw it as essential that the United States find a solution that would offer each government enough concessions to avoid their fall from power. Presumably, the fall of either government could lead to the establishment of an administration less friendly to the United States. Haig said, "Just as Thatcher must show that the junta got nothing for its use of force, Galtieri must be able to show that he got something." The Argentines had to be permitted a more favorable outcome than the status quo ante. To a certain extent, this conflicted with Haig's goal of seeing that aggression was not rewarded, but he saw no alternative if he desired to obtain a peaceful resolution.[18]

DISCUSSION QUESTIONS

1. *What are the costs and benefits of shuttle diplomacy in this case?*
2. *How could Haig strike a balance between the positions of the parties?*
3. *What leverage did the United States have to compel the parties to settle the conflict peacefully?*
4. *What are the short-term risks and longer-term costs of avoiding war? Of failing in the mediation effort?*

BREAKING THE DEADLOCK

The position gradually developed by the U.S. mediators was about midway between the extremes of the "all-British" position and the "balanced" one. The draft, which they showed to both governments, emphasized the following four main points:

1. The British fleet would halt 1,000 miles from the islands, simultaneously with Argentine withdrawal.
2. The islands would be secured by a peacekeeping force made up of the United States, Canada, and two Latin American countries.
3. The same countries would administer the islands, at least for an interim period.
4. Sovereignty would be negotiated later, mediated by the United States.[19]

In Britain, Haig found considerable resentment against the U.S. "evenhanded" stance. Prime Minister Thatcher personally lectured Haig on the challenge that Argentine lawlessness posed to the reputation of the whole Western world and on the importance for Britain and the United States of meeting that challenge.[20] Faced with this British hostility, no serious effort was made by the United States to put real pressure on Britain.

At first Thatcher insisted on unconditional Argentine withdrawal, but Haig, in conjunction with more moderate voices within the British government, brought her around to a tentative acceptance of most of the proposals. However, she still objected that the interim control plans were too vague and insisted that any administration of the islands must possess a "recognizably British" character. Haig's objections and his assertion that he must be able to offer the Argentinians something to enable their government to survive brought no response. Ambassador Henderson's formulation was typical: He responded, "It was not our purpose to help Galtieri survive."[21]

Just as the British insisted that they could concede nothing, Galtieri insisted that Argentina must get something: "The Argentinian government is willing to find a solution that will save Mrs. Thatcher's government, but we cannot sacrifice our honor. You will understand that the Argentinian government has to look good, too."[22] Their absolute minimum requirement was to arrive at some type of formula that would guarantee Argentinian sovereignty. The deadline for this accomplishment was 31 December 1982.

Faced with these conflicting demands and time constraints, the U.S. team made much greater efforts to put pressure on the junta than on Thatcher. Their main approach entailed warning the Argentinians of the danger of their position and attempting to convince the junta members that British resolve to fight was firmer than they imagined, although the mediators initially refrained from predicting Argentine military defeat for fear of insulting and alienating the junta. These warnings had no effect, so the U.S. team soon increased the pressure by warning that the United States, bound by public opinion and its special ties to Britain, would inevitably be compelled to support Britain in case of conflict.

However, such pressure had very little impact on Argentinian perceptions. Galtieri's response, typical of the junta, was "Why are you telling me this? The British won't fight."[23] The Argentinians were baffled by Haig's increasingly rigid stance. They had been prepared for some U.S. criticism, but they also expected to be treated with some degree of deference as a loyal friend of the United States. Shortly after the invasion, an Argentine radio news broadcast said that President Reagan's attempt to dissuade Galtieri from invading was a "logical . . . attempt to preserve [U.S.] relations with the United Kingdom" but that Argentina could expect equally balanced consideration.[24]

However, as Haig's approach diverged further and further from the Argentinians' expectations, their anger at "U.S. duplicity" mounted. Speaking to Vernon Walters, junta member and air force chief Basilio Lami Dozo complained, "I don't understand the attitude of the Washington government. Since well before 2 April you knew that you could count on us in all world theatres, and that if the hemisphere had been threatened you could have used not only the islands but also the continental land mass."[25]

While the mediation team shuttled, the U.S. government back in Washington was hardly united. Despite Haig's concern to maintain an even-handed stance, by mid-April the United States was, *unknown to Haig,* already supplying Britain with not only intelligence but also material aid of various kinds, including aviation fuel, Sidewinder air-to-air missiles, and communications equipment. Defense Secretary Weinberger, concerned about the consequences of possible British defeat, cleared the weapons transfers with Reagan without informing the State Department or the NSC. The junta heard rumors and confronted Haig, who, not surprisingly, denied them.[26] However, from this point on 17 April, Haig's credibility was in question with some of the junta members, especially navy head Admiral Anaya, who lost all trust in Haig and began to treat him as a de facto British agent.

At the same time, in New York Ambassador Kirkpatrick continued to describe the United States as essentially neutral. On 11 April, she told a reporter that although the United States opposed Argentina's use of force, it would not take sides on the ownership issue and had never recognized Britain's claim to the islands. She predicted that the chances for a peaceful settlement were good because the Argentine leaders were willing to negotiate "everything except sovereignty." She also met several times with Argentine officials in New York, assuring them that the United States would not take sides against them.[27]

These assurances had a major impact on Argentine attitudes. Believing that Kirkpatrick, not Haig, represented President Reagan's views, they did not take Haig's threats seriously. In fact, when on 18 April Haig delivered his strongest threats to the junta, warning that the United States would not tolerate Thatcher's fall and would line up with Britain unless Argentina withdrew, in accordance with Resolution 502, Admiral Anaya challenged Haig and told him face-to-face that he was lying.[28]

Despite the deteriorating atmosphere and the erosion of Haig's credibility, some progress toward an agreement was made. A new U.S. proposal for an interim government to be run jointly by Britain and Argentina, with U.S. participation, drew at least British agreement. Also, the British agreed to a 31 December deadline for completing negotiations, although they still insisted on self-determination for the islanders.

For their part, however, the Argentinians did not seem to be able to negotiate in good faith. Throughout the negotiations, concessions would be made and then withdrawn hours or days later. On the 10th, Galtieri agreed to a version of Haig's interim control arrangements, with slight modifications to increase the Argentine symbolic presence, but the next morning Argentine negotiator Costa Mendez made new demands, effectively canceling the areas of agreement that been reached. The same pattern recurred during Haig's second visit on 18-19 April. Haig complained about the Argentinian vacillations, observing that "apparently, some invisible force held the power of veto over the duly constituted authorities of government."[29]

Evidently, every decision could be vetoed by other high officers of the army, navy, and air force, whom the U.S. mediators had no method of contacting. Although Haig believed that he eventually convinced Galtieri of the gravity of Argentina's military and diplomatic positions, Galtieri finally explained to Haig that he had little freedom to make decisions and to control the course of events, saying, "If I lay it all on the line, I won't be here." Haig responded by asking him how long he thought he would last if he lost a war.[30]

In the United States, public opinion had become a significant factor in the determination of policy since the first round of policy discussions. In the Senate, a resolution was introduced that called for U.S. support of Britain and the public sentiment strongly favored the British.

DISCUSSION QUESTIONS

1. *Haig was quite discouraged at this point because he could see that "the fleet was approaching faster than a solution." Several options were available to the mediation team at this point.*
   a. *One option would be to reestablish confidence with the Argentinians by backing off on the threats that had been issued and rely on time, the bite of the EEC sanctions, and the approach of the British fleet to soften the junta's determination. At the same time, the United States would seek more serious concessions from Britain that would give the Argentinians more basis for hope on the sovereignty issue.*
   b. *Another option would be to try to gain more time for negotiations by pressuring the British to slow the advance of their fleet. No one questioned that otherwise negotiations would have to be wrapped up in just a few more days, before the British ships arrived and the shooting started. Haig had raised this issue with the British earlier but then dropped it when Thatcher was adamantly opposed. To succeed, this proposal would depend on convincing the British that negotiations still held real prospects, and it would probably require making at least part of the U.S. stance contingent on such a delay.*
   c. *Third, the mediation could be abandoned. As Haig saw it, this would mean finally going ahead with all the diplomatic and material support for Britain that had been discussed.*
   Which would you advise and why?
4. *How did the U.S. role as third-party mediator in the Falklands/Malvinas crisis differ or compare to that in the Suez crisis? Did U.S. mediation inevitably promote or hinder the achievement of peace? How did the cast of characters compare in both cases of mediation?*

NOTES

1. Wideawake was the closest usable airfield to the Falklands and was needed especially as a staging area and transshipment point. Ascension is a British possession, but the base is U.S.; the original treaty gives Britain

"emergency use" rights, but they would need much more for active military operations.

2. *New York Times*, 8 April 1982, p. A-10; *Economist*, 3 March 1984, pp. 29-31.

3. Alexander Haig, *Caveat: Realism, Reagan, and Foreign Policy* (New York: Macmillan, 1984), pp. 268-269; Max Hastings and Simon Jenkins, *The Falklands War* (New York: Norton, 1983), p. 104; *New York Times*, 8 April 1982, p. A-10.

4. David Feldman, "The U.S. Role in the Malvinas Crisis, 1982," *Journal of Interamerican Studies and World Affairs* 27, no. 2 (Summer 1985), pp. 7-8. Hastings and Jenkins, *The Falklands War*, p. 103.

5. Haig, *Caveat*, p. 269.

6. Haig, *Caveat*, p. 267; *New York Times*, 8 April 1982, p. A-10.

7. Haig, *Caveat*, p. 266.

8. Interview with Lawrence Eagleburger by Chaim D. Kaufmann.

9. Interview with Bobby Inman by Chaim D. Kaufmann.

10. Argentina retained at least the rhetorical support of virtually all other Latin American countries throughout the crisis. In addition Peru and Bolivia made offers to contribute forces and Brazil offered to sell equipment, but there is no evidence that any of them actually did so.

11. In fact, British opinion was not united at first. In Parliament, a number of Labor members of Parliament (MPs) doubted both the appropriateness and the prospects of resorting to force. Tony Benn's reaction was typical: "I [told] the Prime Minister that this is an ill-thought-out enterprise and will not achieve the purposes to which it is put. By acting that way, she has already lost much of the support that was carefully garnered for the Security Council resolution [on 3 April]" (Parliamentary Debates (Commons), *The Falklands Campaign*, 7 April, p. 44).

However, it quickly became apparent that the task force had the support of the majority of the population; a mid-April poll showed that 60 percent supported Thatcher's hard line. Labor party leaders, unwilling to be branded unpatriotic in a time of national crisis, nearly all joined in solidarity with the government.

12. Hastings and Jenkins, *The Falklands War*, p. 113; Sir Nicholas Henderson, "America and the Falklands: Case Study in the Behaviour of an Ally," *Economist*, 12 November 1983, p. 32.

13. Haig, *Caveat*, p. 271.

14. Haig, *Caveat*, pp. 272-274, 279; Henderson, "America and the Falklands," p. 32; Feldman, "The U.S. Role," pp. 15-16.

15. David C. Gompert, "American Diplomacy and the Haig Mission: An Insider's Perspective," in Alberto Coll and Anthony Arend, eds., *The Falklands War: Lessons for Strategy, Diplomacy, and International Law* (Boston: George, Allen & Unwin, 1985), p. 111.

16. Haig, *Caveat*, p. 278. "Another army" referred to Britain's attempt to capture Buenos Aires in 1806-1807, which failed miserably.

17. Haig, *Caveat*, pp. 274-275, 278, 281-282; *New York Times*, 17 April 1982, p. 5; Douglas Kinney, "Anglo-Argentine Diplomacy and the Falklands Crisis," in Coll and Arend, *The Falklands War*, p. 90.

18. Haig, *Caveat*, p. 274; Gompert, "American Diplomacy," p. 112; Henderson, "America and the Falklands," p. 33.

19. Haig, *Caveat*, pp. 271-274.

20. Haig, *Caveat*, pp. 273-274; Henderson, "America and the Falklands," pp. 32-33; Hastings and Jenkins, *The Falklands War*, p. 107.

21. Henderson, "America and the Falklands," p. 32.

22. Haig, *Caveat*, p. 277.

23. Haig, *Caveat*, p. 280.

24. *Noticias Argentinas*, 5 April 1982, translated in *FBIS*, vol. 6, no. 65, p. B-5.

25. Alejandro Dabat and Luis Lorenzano, *Argentina: The Malvinas and the End of Military Rule* (London: Verso, 1984), p. 79 n. 18.

26. Haig, *Caveat*, p. 285.

27. Reports of these meetings drew very strong protests from the British. *New York Times*, 12 April 1982, p. A-10; Haig, *Caveat*, p. 269; Feldman, "The U.S. Role in the Malvinas Crisis," p. 7.

28. Feldman, "The U.S. Role in the Malvinas Crisis," pp. 7, 9, 11-12; Hastings and Jenkins, *The Falklands War*, p. 111.

29. Haig, *Caveat*, pp. 286-287.

30. Haig, *Caveat*, pp. 286-289.

FURTHER READING ON
THE FALKLANDS/MALVINAS WAR

Coll, Alberto R., and Anthony C. Arend eds. *The Falklands War*. Boston: George, Allen and Unwin, 1985.

Dabat, Alejandro, and Luis Lorenzano. *Argentina: The Malvinas and the End of Military Rule*, translated by Ralph Johnstone. Thetford, Norfolk: The Thetford Press Limited, 1984.

Freedman, Lawrence and Virginia Gamba-Stonehouse. *Signals of War*. Boston: Faber and Faber, 1990.

Gamba, Virginia. *The Falklands/Malvinas War*. Boston: Allen and Unwin, Inc., 1987.

Gustafson, Lowell S. *The Sovereignty Dispute over the Falklands (Malvinas) Islands*. London: Oxford University Press, 1988.

Kinney, Douglas. *National Interest, National Honor: The Diplomacy of the Falklands Crisis*. New York: Praeger, 1989.

6

RESOLVING THE
LEBANON CRISIS, 1982–1983

On 6 June 1982, the Israeli Defense Forces, or IDF, moved across Israel's northern border into Lebanon. According to Prime Minister Menachem Begin and Defense Minister Ariel Sharon, "Operation Peace for Galilee" was intended to neutralize fighting units of the Palestine Liberation Organization (PLO) and to drive them far enough back from the Israeli border to prevent further harassment of Israel's northernmost settlements with rocket and artillery fire. The drive, Israel assured the U.S. government, would stop 40 kilometers, some 27 miles, into Lebanon.

Despite Israeli promises, however, the IDF continued to move north for a week until it had encircled Beirut, Lebanon's capital and a PLO stronghold. It became clear that Israel's real goals were far more ambitious: to break the PLO's military back permanently and to install a friendly regime in Beirut, with hopes of cultivating Lebanon as the second Arab state (after Anwar Sadat's Egypt) to sign a peace treaty with Israel. These goals, or at least Israel's use of main force to achieve them, were far more difficult for the United States to accept. In response, the Reagan administration suspended a recently signed Memorandum of Strategic Understanding, with which it had formed a loose military alliance with Israel, and dispatched veteran diplomat and negotiator Philip Habib to Lebanon to defuse the crisis.

This chapter is an edited version of the case study by Richard Haas and David Kennedy, The Reagan Administration and Lebanon, *Pew case study no. 340.*

The political environment Habib faced was enormously complicated. Lebanon had long been a cockpit of internal and regional tension. Its politics have been dominated by struggles, often armed, between Christians, particularly the strong Maronite sect and its Phalange militia, and Moslems, especially the Druze and Shiite sects and their militias. Lebanon's government was based on an informal compact dating from 1943, known as the National Pact, which reflected the population distributions of the past. Christians had then been a majority in the country; thus the pact stipulated that the Lebanese president would be Maronite and provided for a slim 6 to 5 Maronite majority in the parliament in order to guarantee Christian predominance. On the other hand, the prime minister would be a Sunni Moslem and the Speaker of the House a Shiite Moslem, thus ensuring the Arab-Moslem character of the nation. Since 1943, the Christians had become a minority, but they had prevented any new consensus taking and refused to cede or share power. The political situation was further complicated by the presence of several hundred thousand displaced Palestinians, including some well-armed and well-financed PLO members, who had settled in Lebanon because of its proximity to Israel. No single Lebanese Christian faction was strong enough to drive them out. The Palestinians took over a large portion of southern Lebanon, made common and often violent cause with Lebanon's Moslems against the Christians, and launched artillery and commando raids into Israel.

The Israelis had amassed a long list of past territorial victories in wars against several Arab states. In May 1948, Lebanon, Jordan, Egypt, Syria, Saudi Arabia, and Iraq aided the Palestinians and initiated a war to prevent the formation of an Israeli state. As a result of this war, Israel managed to seize additional land, which had been reserved by the U.N. for incorporation into a proposed Palestinian state. However, Palestinian attacks were continually launched against Israel from bases in nearby Arab territories. In retaliation, Israel struck against Egypt, Jordan, and Syria in 1967 and accomplished the eventual Israeli occupation of the Sinai Peninsula, Golan Heights, and West Bank territories.

In 1975, Lebanon's simmering religious and political tension erupted into full-fledged civil war as a result of an increasing Palestinian population in Lebanon and escalating tensions between Christians and Moslems. The fighting was vicious, involving atrocities on both sides. The Christians, unable to handle both Lebanon's Moslems and their Palestinian allies, ultimately invited Syria's President Hafez Assad to send forces, in a desperate attempt to stop the fighting. Assad did so; he sympathized mainly with Lebanon's Moslems, but as regional power broker he was more concerned with preventing the country from becoming an even more powerful Palestinian stronghold. Once in Lebanon, Assad, who had long aspired to annex Lebanon as part of a historical "Greater Syria," never fully withdrew. Although he respected informal "red lines" drawn by Israel in the south, he maintained a garrison in Beirut and occupied much of the country's north and east sectors. The Syrian president, who had strong Soviet ties, continued to support Lebanese Moslem parties and militias to keep the Christians weak and off balance. The Palestinians remained strong, and Israel eventually responded to the PLO's military harassment by seizing a belt of Lebanon just north of their common border and placing it under the control of Colonel Saad Haddad, a renegade Lebanese army officer sympathetic to Israel. In the early 1980s, PLO raids dropped off considerably because of a combination of Israel's measures and a PLO attempt to move toward political respectability.

Internal Lebanese factional maneuvering continued, however, and a leading Maronite and Phalangist, Bashir Gemayel, developed strong ties to Israel. Gemayel hinted at an attractive proposition: If Israel would move into Lebanon and subdue the Palestinians (and perhaps even the Syrians) and help install him as president, he would ensure that the PLO stayed toothless in the long run and would eventually consider the prospect of signing a peace treaty with Israel (Lebanon, like all other Arab states except Egypt, had technically been at war with Israel since 1948). Although the PLO's cross-border attacks had largely abated, Begin and Sharon were determined to finish the PLO and assure a friendly Lebanon. Operation Peace for Galilee, long planned and prepared, was unleashed after an assassination attempt against an Israeli ambassador in London (the terrorists belonged to a Palestinian splinter group so hostile to the PLO that Yasser Arafat had put a price on its leader's head). The Israeli advance was resisted by the PLO and the Syrians, but to little avail. The Palestinians were beaten back, and the Syrians signed a cease-fire after Israel, in what was widely regarded as a stunning military tour de force, destroyed that country's extensive Soviet-supplied air-defense system in Lebanon and shot down a quarter of its air force. In an attempt to destroy or drive out the PLO, Israel laid devastating siege to Beirut, cutting off power and water to Moslem West Beirut and pounding the city with heavy artillery and air strikes over strong U.S. protests.

At this point, President Reagan instructed Ambassador Habib to prevent the situation from unraveling and to try to bring about a cease-fire. Habib's party included veteran U.S. diplomat Morris Draper. According to one State Department official working with the team, the United States wanted

> an arrangement where the Israelis would withdraw from Lebanon in return for adequate security arrangements, meaning that southern Lebanon would have to be free of arms. We wanted to control or, ideally, forestall, through cease-fires or other arrangements, major fighting between Syria and Israel, because we couldn't tell where that would go. And we were thinking that we would like to see a Lebanon able to take care of its own country, end the kind of civil war that had

been going on. Get the foreigners out of their country, and try to turn things over to the Lebanese. That was the most ambitious objective of all, because the Lebanese are so weak and divided.

REACHING THE DECISION TO NEGOTIATE

Late in August, after a series of abortive cease-fires, Habib eventually managed to broker a deal that ended the siege of Beirut. The PLO, for its part, would surrender its heavy weapons to the Lebanese government and evacuate its 15,000 military personnel in Beirut; some 3,400 would go by ship to various Arab ports, the balance overland to Syria. Israel, for its part, would let them go. A key component of the bargain was a U.S. guarantee that Palestinian civilians, who remained in settlements ("camps") in the Beirut area, would not be harmed by Lebanese militias or by Israel once their military protectors were gone.

A multinational force (MNF) of U.S. marines, French forces, and Italian forces was brought into Beirut as the PLO's soldiers prepared to leave. As early as the end of June, according to the State Department official with Habib's party, it had been clear that "we couldn't get an agreement unless there was some kind of international force" involved. The PLO was concerned that its enemies, Lebanese and Israeli, would strike against its soldiers as they assembled to depart Beirut and insisted that a peacekeeping force be brought in to supervise the withdrawal (Arafat initially rejected U.S. participation in such a force because of U.S. ties with Israel but later reconsidered). The beleaguered Lebanese, the U.S. official said, were anxious for some sign of international commitment to their country's integrity and felt that "troops on the scene would help. When people do something as drastic as putting troops into a combat zone, that's a very strong commitment that the governments that do that are going to stick with it."

Ambassador Habib and his party also wanted U.S. troops in Lebanon. There was never any intent to involve the marines in the actual fighting, although Habib did think that U.S. troops might prevent further conflict by strategically patrolling Beirut or placing marines at checkpoints throughout the city to guard against, for instance, the movement of arms. The goal of the U.S. presence, as with the PLO evacuation, was to encourage belligerent parties to enter into agreements and to ensure that the terms were enacted. Religious militias might, for instance, surrender control of turf to the central government in exchange for guarantees of government protection from other militias.

Habib's views were shared strongly by the National Security Council (NSC), then under the direction of national security adviser and long-time presidential confidant William "Judge" Clark. "The idea was that the effort would be a real assertion of superpower strength," said then-NSC Middle East staffer Geoffrey Kemp.

Secretary of Defense Caspar Weinberger and the Pentagon, however, did not share this activist outlook. "The Pentagon fought as hard as it could for as limited a role as possible," said Francis J. "Bing" West, then assistant secretary of defense for international security affairs.

> The Department of Defense didn't want our troops going in at all in that situation. There wasn't a military mission. It's difficult to talk with a military man when you want to talk about political symbolism. We could understand why people might want us there as a symbol and a guarantee, but a symbol and guarantee of what? It wasn't peace-keeping; there wasn't really a peace to keep.

Although Weinberger was not able to persuade President Reagan to keep the United States out of the MNF, the Pentagon did manage to impose strict limits on the marines' mission. They would stay in Beirut for a maximum of thirty days, instead of the sixty days Habib had asked for, and would be restricted to the city's port area. The president also made public assurances that the marines would be withdrawn if fired upon. Although Habib was glad to obtain the marines' protection for the evacuation, the limited U.S. deployment did not inspire the level of confidence within Lebanon that the envoy had anticipated. "The Palestinians wanted the force to stay for a lot longer, and the Lebanese were very unhappy: they wanted us to stay a minimum of two months," said the State Department official with Habib's party.

The MNF arrived in Beirut on 25 August 1982, and the PLO evacuation occurred without incident between the 28th and the 31st. On 14 September, the marines were called home. "DOD pushed to get the MNF to leave precipitously," a State Department official said. "They were out two weeks before anybody expected them to be." Secretary Weinberger had visited Beirut and consequently made it clear to Habib and his party that he advocated a swift departure of the U.S. Marine forces. Habib bowed to the inevitable.

In Washington, the marines' withdrawal was a shock to the administration's foreign policy community. "As far as I know, there was no interagency process, no working groups that decided, all right, we'll pull out now," said a ranking State Department official.

> There wasn't anything in this sense that was communicated. On the contrary, what I remember is that Weinberger actually makes a public statement that they're out, and everybody's pretty much taken by

surprise. Whether he told the President or not I don't know, but I don't know of anybody else who knew about it.

One reason why Habib and his party had given their reluctant approval to the marine evacuation was that, at the time, Beirut appeared to be relatively calm and under control. On 23 August, the Lebanese parliament had elected Maronite Christian strongman Bashir Gemayel president. "Bashir had given us a promise that we could believe," said the State Department official with Habib, "that the Palestinians [civilians left in Beirut] were not going to be assassinated, and that the Phalange was not going to run wild. We had his faithful promise: he owed the Americans so much."

The United States had, indeed, joined Israel in strongly backing Gemayel's candidacy, not only supporting his leadership but even arranging details of transportation and security for Moslem members of parliament, who feared factional reprisal should they vote for the Maronite. The United States (Habib and his party) believed that "he was the key to the long-term plan" to put Lebanon back together, said the State Department official. "We saw him as the most promising leader: although he'd done some outrageous things, he had a type of charisma and determination and flexibility that would allow him to take over the country." The U.S. diplomats had encouraged Gemayel to build new bridges to Lebanon's most important Moslem groups as a crucial first step toward building new national cohesion. "The Shiite and Druze leadership, despite their reservations, came on board," the official said. "Very reluctantly, but it was enough." Viewed in that context, Habib's party thought that it was probably safe to allow the MNF to return home.

Bashir Gemayel was also the key to carrying out Habib's plan to remove all foreign forces from Lebanon. He had, the United States felt, a proper and realistic attitude toward his powerful neighbors. "He was not letting himself be caught up too closely with the Israelis, but he wanted to maintain a good relationship with them, and he was willing to make them a square deal on security arrangements," the official said.

That was what we wanted, too. He hated the Syrians, he wanted the Syrians out of his country—as we did—but I think he was willing to offer the Syrians certain guarantees that the Syrians were concerned about, and to make sure that there was a friendly relationship between the governments in Beirut and Damascus.

Based on these developments, the United States felt that the time was ripe for arranging rapid Israeli and Syrian withdrawals. "Our self-imposed deadline was the end of 1982," the official said. The Syrians had suffered great military humiliation at Israel's hands, and Habib wanted to move before those memories began to dim. From an Israeli perspective, the war was expensive and increasingly unpopular. The United States had high hopes that a newly, if tentatively, cohesive Lebanon under Bashir Gemayel could, with strong U.S. backing, put all the pieces together.

DISCUSSION QUESTIONS

1. *Which of the parties to the conflict wanted to avoid negotiating at this point?*
2. *Of those parties, which appeared to favor negotiations? What objectives did they have in common?*
3. *What gave the United States leverage in this situation to influence the parties? What did not?*
4. *What could derail the process?*

GETTING TO THE TABLE

On the afternoon of 14 September, the same day the MNF embarked from Beirut, Gemayel was assassinated at Phalange headquarters, allegedly at Syrian direction. The Israeli army, ignoring U.S. protests, moved into the city. Within days, the IDF permitted Phalangist militiamen to invade two Palestinian camps in the city, Sabra and Shatilla, where the Phalangists murdered some 700 civilians in reprisal for Gemayel's death. The MNF nations, horrified that the U.S. guarantees of Palestinian safety had been so dramatically violated, prepared to move their forces back into Beirut.

Once again, the Pentagon was extremely nervous about getting involved in a vaguely defined mission in Lebanon, but it did not actively oppose the deployment at this time. Military authorities did, however, limit it. At Pentagon insistence, marines were deployed at Beirut International Airport, which afforded a convenient location for resupply or evacuation operations. The airport, overshadowed by the high ground of the Shouf Mountains just to the south, was tactically insecure ground. This vulnerability appealed to some in the military because posting the marines there would signal to potential Lebanese combatants that the United States had no intention of fighting. The marines' mission order was drafted by the joint chiefs of staff in such a way as to avoid giving the marines even implicit responsibility for protecting either the airport or any other part of Beirut. The order also directed that the marines would not engage in combat, unless self-defense made it unavoidable, and that the U.S. commander in chief in Europe (based in Stuttgart, West Germany) should be prepared to evacuate them if required by hostile action.

The Pentagon was unsuccessful in imposing a deadline on the deployment. Habib's strategy was to use the MNF to strengthen Lebanon's hand while he brokered the speedy withdrawal of Syrian and Israeli forces. His message was that the job would take two months: Nicholas A. Veliotes, assistant secretary of state for Near Eastern and South Asian affairs, told the House Foreign Affairs Committee late in September that the end of 1982 was the "outer limit" of the marines' stay in Lebanon. The diplomats refused to be pinned down formally, however. "We tried to make it explicit that we were only going in for 60 days," said Assistant Secretary of Defense West.

> I tried to have that written into the operations order. And people at my level over in State sort of said, "now look, you're really trying to hold our feet to the fire: it might be 65 days, it might be 55 days. You've got to give us some latitude on this." And I said, "hey, in essence, we don't mean years." And they said, "of course we don't mean years."

The MNF returned to Beirut on 29 September. Its presence alone restored an uneasy peace; no shots were fired. Bashir's brother Amin was elected president in his stead. But with the marines in Beirut and matters once more under control, at least temporarily, the Reagan administration faced the difficult question of what to do next.

President Reagan publicly set forth U.S. goals in a television speech shortly after the marines returned: The MNF was in Beirut to support the withdrawal of "all foreign forces"—Syrian and Israeli—from Lebanon and to assist in Lebanese state building. These were, of course, the same goals that Habib had advocated (and that the Defense Department had opposed) when the envoy first proposed U.S. military involvement back in June. In September Reagan finally made them stick.

By all accounts, the envoy, backed by President Reagan and the newly appointed secretary of state, George Shultz, exercised nearly unalloyed primacy. During this period of time, Habib was the key player. Habib maintained that diplomatic priority should be given to brokering an Israeli disengagement agreement with Lebanon. He believed that Syria would voluntarily withdraw following an Israel departure. This belief was "premised," said a senior White House official, "upon Saudi statements, and winks and nods, that yes, we know—we the Saudis—that when you get Israeli withdrawal, you will get Syrian withdrawal, and that Syria has no greater ambitions vis-à-vis Lebanon." Habib and Shultz also believed that the United States could rely on moderate Arab—chiefly Saudi—pressure to move Assad when the time came. Thus, Syria was generally informed of U.S. activities to promote the disengagement negotiations but not invited to supply opinions on the issues or to participate in talks over the precise details of an agreement.

Habib argued vigorously that an agreement between Israel and Lebanon could be obtained in as little as six weeks, certainly before Christmas. Israel was in political shock over the massacres of civilians in the Palestinian camps of Sabra and Shatilla, and there was mounting opposition to the war and to the casualties the IDF was taking in continuing skirmishes. Habib believed that the Begin administration would be willing to accept a plan of politically strategic withdrawal.

On 1 September, as the PLO sailed away from Beirut, President Reagan announced what came to be called the Reagan Plan, intended to function as a major step in the peace process. The plan, which essentially built on and explicated aspects of the Camp David Accords, called on Jordan's King Hussein to negotiate with Israel on behalf of the Palestinians, probably for some kind of Jordanian-administered entity in the Israeli-occupied West Bank. The United States tendered the plan in a simultaneous desire to capitalize on what it regarded as a great success (the U.S.-brokered PLO withdrawal, which underscored U.S. influence in the region) and to distance itself somewhat from Israel, whose conservative Likud government emphatically did not want to surrender the West Bank. Begin rejected the plan outright (which did the United States no harm in Arab eyes) and accelerated the construction of settlements in the occupied territories (the more settlements, the harder for any Israeli government to cede the lands in future negotiations). The Arab countries, however, met in Fez, Morocco, and cautiously endorsed the U.S. proposal; King Hussein, too, showed potential willingness to negotiate with Israel if he could secure Arafat's backing to do so. These were very encouraging signs, leading the Reagan administration and the Arab world to hope that some progress could finally be made in the region.

The marines' return to Lebanon, and President Reagan's explicit commitment of U.S. power and prestige to getting Syria and Israel out of the country quickly, were immediately and inevitably linked to the international maneuvering surrounding the Reagan Plan. "Nobody mistook the importance of whatever happened in Lebanon to the larger picture," said an administration official. "People who were trying to decide whether to take risks [in the peace process], like King Hussein, would—whether we liked it or not—be impressed one way or another by what happened in Lebanon."

In December, Hussein came to Washington to talk about the peace process. One of several conditions he laid down for his participation was that there be meaningful and rapid progress on Israeli withdrawal from Lebanon. Once again, it was emphasized that until the Israelis were out, the Reagan Plan was worthless, and that if the United States could broker such a withdrawal, one satisfactory to the moderate Arabs, U.S. credibility in the larger peace process would be enormously increased. There was speculation in the United States that Begin was deliberately drawing out negotiations precisely in order to scuttle the peace process.

The completion of the Lebanon talks was in fact nowhere in sight: By late November Israel and Lebanon had been unable to agree on preliminary issues, such as an agenda or a site for negotiations, much less on an actual withdrawal agreement. The agenda Israel had floated earlier in the month was secret, but according to the well-connected *Middle East Policy Survey* (MEPS), Israel wanted an end to the state of war between the two countries; a prohibition on stationing of foreign forces in Lebanon without Israeli consent; a ban on Lebanon's participation in hostilities in alliance with a third party; Lebanon's permission to place Israeli observation posts, or early warning stations, deep within Lebanon; and a 45-kilometer (27-mile) buffer zone inside of Lebanon's southern border, to be jointly patrolled by Israeli and Haddad's troops.

Israel also asked for "normalization of relations," which included open borders, mutual diplomatic representation, free trade agreements, and other features. Finally, it insisted that the talks be held, at least in part, in Jerusalem, in effect requiring the Gemayel government to endorse Israel's position that the contested Holy City was under Israeli sovereignty. "Begin was on the ropes over Sabra and Shatilla and the unpopularity of the war," former NSC staff member Geoffrey Kemp said, giving the NSC's analysis of the Israeli agenda. "Therefore if he agreed to a premature withdrawal with no goodies, i.e., diplomatic relations and trade access, the whole war in Lebanon would have seemed a waste. So Begin and Sharon were hanging on for a really good deal."

Lebanon seemed a long way from giving in. The Lebanese position reportedly began with an insistence that it would abandon talks entirely rather than travel to Jerusalem. The Gemayel government was also wary of offending its internal opponents and Arab neighbors by undertaking talks—like normalization talks—which resembled full-fledged peace negotiations. It preferred to open discussions on purely military topics, such as an Israeli withdrawal and issues of border security, with a military official negotiating for the Lebanese. They then proposed to "discover" the nonmilitary issues in the course of negotiating, whereupon a ranking civilian could be enlisted to take over. Conversely, Israel opposed the strategy, although they wanted just as strongly to underscore the political nature of the talks in order to emphasize that Lebanon was dealing with it as a legitimate nation rather than simply an occupying army.

Gemayel's Moslem prime minister, Shafiq Wazzan, reportedly preferred a long-term Israeli occupation to normalization and wanted to clear each issue to be taken up in the disengagement talks with other Arab governments. The United States viewed this approach as a prescription for stagnation. Machinations within the Lebanese government became so chaotic and polarized that at one point Gemayel, in secret talks, reached agreement with Sharon on an agenda for subsequent negotiations, then had Habib present it to Wazzan to disguise his own role (Wazzan rejected the agenda). Saad Haddad was a sticking point; the Lebanese regarded him as a turncoat and loathed the idea of finding him a new official role instead of punishing him.

The Israeli security proposals, such as posts on Lebanese ground and patrols on Lebanon's side of the border, were anathema, if not to Gemayel himself then to the Moslem opposition he could not afford to offend too deeply.

While Habib and his party shuttled inconclusively between Lebanon and Israel, attempting to initiate talks, the U.S. foreign policy apparatus grappled with the question of what to do in the meantime and how to proceed if he succeeded. The most insistent issue was defining the role of the marines at the airport in Beirut. "There was this continuing drumfire from the Pentagon," said a mid-level State Department official.

> What good is it to have the Marines there? What are they there for? We spent a lot of time trying to convince them that we had a political strategy of which the Marines were a part. It was hard, because it had been decided at the very highest levels of the U.S. government that they would be an integral part, and it was always a given that they had to have a major role—but nobody had figured out what it should be.

The U.S. military, at this point and throughout, resisted any expansion of the marines' role. "There was a very rigid approach which said, we've got the Marines there at the airport, let's leave them there, let's try to get them out," said General E. C. "Shy" Meyer, then the army chief of staff.

> The Chiefs saw a situation in which there was no clear identification of mission, in which there was no clear identification of interests, in which there was no clear identification of what role the military was intended to play. No one in the administration, from the State Department through the White House, was able to explain the purpose of the force there.

By contrast, Habib, in conjunction with the senior officials of the State Department and the NSC, aggressively promoted the assumption of a more active role for the marines and the MNF.

Secretary of Defense Weinberger felt strongly that the United States now needed to lean on Israel. In the discussions that Habib was holding with Israel and Lebanon, Israel was still holding out for what amounted to a peace treaty and full diplomatic relations, thus postponing the Israeli withdrawal (and, by implication, the Syrian withdrawal) indefinitely. Toward the end of 1982, there were indeed signs that the administration was becoming frustrated enough with the stagnation in Lebanon to try to pressure Israel somewhat. President Reagan sent a message to the Subcommittee on Foreign Affairs of the House Appropriations Committee that asked it to reject a congressionally inspired plan to boost aid to Israel, in contradiction to the administration's request, and argued that the increase would reward Israeli "intransigence."

Rumors also reached the press that a suspension of arms aid was contemplated.

DISCUSSION QUESTIONS

1. *What leverage had the United States used to get the parties to agree to some form of negotiation?*
2. *What additional pressure was required to hasten the process? At what cost was it to the United States objectives in the Middle East?*
3. *On which parties did progress in negotiations now depend?*

BREAKING THE DEADLOCK

Other key players, as it turned out, had not written themselves out of the Middle East drama. The Syrians and the Soviets, jointly humiliated by Israel's stunning military successes earlier in the year, began to take part again toward the end of 1982. One of the first signs was a massive infusion of some $2 billion worth of Soviet military equipment into Syria. Chief among the new gear were top-of-the-line Soviet SAM-5 antiaircraft missiles, complete with Soviet crews, of sufficient range and effectiveness to cover all of Lebanon and reach into northern Israel. Assad had been weakened in his region, and his Lebanese clients weakened in Lebanese politics, by Syria's ineffectiveness in the summer war, but both were uplifted by the U.S.S.R.'s powerful gesture of continued commitment to maintaining Syria as a regional power.

The combination of perceived Syrian aspirations and the increase in their military strength seemed to stack the deck further against the U.S. efforts. Geoffrey Kemp said,

> As the Syrians began to regroup and regain their strength, and the Russians decided that nothing dramatic was going to happen [because of U.S. diplomacy], and that they should start playing the game again, Gemayel began to feel the hot breath of Russia and its allies the Syrians down his neck. It limited his scope to reach a compromise, so that by the end of the year, everyone was exceedingly pessimistic about any hope for compromise.

"This was when you began getting the first discussions at the working level: how long can the MNF stay?" said a mid-level State Department official. "How can you get the United States out? The United States does not wish to be committed here indefinitely."

The one hope, to advocates of an early U.S. departure, lay in an intensive program to enlarge, equip, and train the Lebanese Armed Forces (LAF), bankrolled and managed largely by the United States and begun late in 1982. There were at least three attractive features to this plan. The dominant rationale, and the one that appealed most to the Pentagon, was that if the LAF, in recent years a fairly ineffectual force, could be made larger, more cohesive, and more powerful, it could assume the job of guaranteeing Lebanon's internal security, which might otherwise demand an expanded MNF. Another feature was that the main obstacle to the competence of the LAF was internal conflict and divisions: In a mirror of the larger Lebanese society, most of the LAF's officers were Christians, most of its rank and file Moslem, and it could not be trusted to act either as one body or on behalf of the Maronite-dominated central government. U.S. enthusiasts for building up a strong and effective LAF thought that a successful unifying effort would prove to be a useful military measure as well as a symbolic act illustrating in microcosm the potential for Lebanese society to overcome religious factionalism. Finally, a success would be simply that: a U.S. success, providing an excuse for those in the administration who were anxious to declare victory and withdraw.

At the same time, domestic politics in Israel—especially the reactions triggered by the release of the official Kahan Commission Report on Israeli responsibility for the Sabra and Shatilla massacres—forced Ariel Sharon to relinquish his defense post (he remained in the cabinet, however, as minister without portfolio). He was replaced by Moshe Arens, with whom George Shultz had enjoyed warm relations when the Israeli was ambassador to the United States. Arens indicated a willingness to be flexible in the disengagement negotiations, unlike the abrasive and confrontational Sharon. This leadership change seemed to strengthen Habib's and Shultz' hopes for success in obtaining Israeli withdrawal soon and Syrian withdrawal soon after.

Habib continued to work to find common ground in the disengagement talks although not without raising diplomatic hackles. Shortly after the new year, the special envoy had reportedly prompted Israeli objections by acting, as those objections put it, as an "arbiter" in the talks rather than simply as a "mediator." Habib had sparked the objections by criticizing Israel's comprehensive disengagement-with-normalization agenda, telling Israel that it could, in the words of one account, obtain "security arrangements and a bit of normalization, or nothing." By late February, the Arens-influenced Israeli delegation seemed in fact to be moving in this direction; there were signs that it would settle for a commitment to later normalization talks, rather than insist on concurrent normalization and withdrawal, and that it was moderating its security demands. But Habib evidently still felt that Israel was being unreasonably ambitious and balky, and Israel let it be known in Washington that it did not appreciate its perception of the special envoy's support of Lebanon on key questions or its unfair labeling of Israel as "obstructionist."

Shultz soon began exploring potential incentives to offer the Israelis in order to encourage their withdrawal. By late March 1983, he had directed senior department officials to investigate reviving the suspended Memorandum of Strategic Understanding, to begin work to lift an embargo on the sale of F-16 fighters that dated from Israel's bombing of Iraq's nuclear reactor in June 1981, and to arrange an expedited sale of Sidewinder air-to-air missiles. He and his staff also managed, with considerable difficulty and opposition from the Pentagon, to pry agreement out of the Defense Department to allow Israel access to manufacturing methods for very advanced high-technology airframe materials to be used in Israel's planned Lavi fighter airplane.

If, at this point, there were signs of hope in the Lebanese-Israeli talks, and reason to think that the United States possessed sufficient instruments to influence the outcome, the signs for the Reagan Plan were considerably more mixed. Hussein, simultaneously eager for progress and unwilling to be too exposed for a long period, had imposed a deadline of 1 March 1983 for his decision on whether to enter into regional negotiations. He and Arafat, closely watched by other Arab leaders, were talking about—or perhaps talking about talking about—the conditions under which the Jordanian king might represent the Palestinians in peace talks and the list of participants involved in such talks. Arafat, pressured from within the loosely structured PLO by confrontation-minded radicals, was encountering more Palestinian resistance to working with Hussein than most regional specialists had anticipated. According to the MEPS, whereas once he had been expected to give Hussein a cautious "yellow light" to proceed, he was now expected to give an even less definitive "flashing yellow light." But the prospects still seemed encouraging for some solution. Some proposed means seemed more promising than others, however; the MEPS reported that in one bizarre footnote to the Arab world's complex positioning on the peace process, Saudi Foreign Minister Saud Faisal pressed the United States to provide the PLO with a military base in Egypt as a "sweetener" to enter negotiations. U.S. government officials expected to be able to meet many of the preconditions they anticipated Hussein would impose, such as security guarantees and financial support for Jordan. They were considerably less sanguine regarding their capacity to provide another explicit precondition—an Israeli settlement freeze. Even if they could, it might become neutralized if they could not also deliver an Israeli withdrawal from Lebanon. According to reports, Hussein was not personally preoccupied with Lebanon, but to take the risk of entering negotiations he needed support from Egypt and Saudi Arabia, which were concerned, and dared not offend Syria's Assad.

1 March arrived and departed without either a settlement freeze or a withdrawal. President Reagan, in a move intended to box both Israel and Jordan into moving ahead with negotiations, tried to overcome the obstacle of Israel's continuing and stepped-up settlement construction by promising Hussein that if he would agree, in principle, to enter into negotiations with Israel, he would not actually have to do so until Israel froze construction. U.S. officials continued to hope, but their expectations were fleeting. On 10 April, the Jordanian king announced that he would not enter into regional negotiations either on behalf of the PLO or alone; the Reagan Plan was virtually dead. (Also on 10 April, in a grim reminder of the severity with which disapproval can be expressed in Mideast politics, Isam Sartawi—the most peace-minded member of the PLO leadership and one who had extensive contacts with the like-minded Israelis—was assassinated by Palestinian radicals in Portugal.) A week and a day later, in the first major assault against the United States in Lebanon, the U.S. embassy in Beirut was bombed by terrorists (widely believed, in the United States, to be Syrian-backed). Sixty people were killed.

On 22 April, prompted by Habib's sense that he had closed the gap between Israel and Lebanon sufficiently to merit a final, high-profile push, President Reagan sent Secretary Shultz to the Middle East to obtain "the urgent and total withdrawal" of all foreign forces. The policy of sorting out Lebanese-Israeli relations first, and subsequently attending to Syria, was still in force: Shultz was scheduled to visit Jerusalem, Beirut, and Cairo, with Syria and other Arab states tentatively scheduled for later. "Once a satisfactory agreement is reached," Shultz told the *Washington Post*, "then we have to say to the Syrians, 'All right, the Israelis have agreed to withdraw, now it's up to you,' and try to work out some kind of schedule." Shultz and Habib remained convinced that the most promising strategy would be the orchestration of regional leverage to secure Syrian cooperation. However, ominous signs were surfacing, indicating increasing Soviet pressure on Assad to take a hard line against withdrawal.

On Wednesday, 4 May, the Gemayel government accepted Shultz's proposal for the withdrawal of Israeli forces, and the secretary of state flew to Jerusalem, where the signs were positive, to try to win Israeli acquiescence. The main elements of the agreement were that each country would respect the sovereignty and territorial integrity of the other; the state of war between the two countries was terminated. Israel would withdraw its armed forces from Lebanon in accordance with a secret annex to the agreement (which was widely believed to provide for joint Israeli-Lebanese patrols in southern Lebanon); the two countries would settle disputes between them by peaceful means; both would pursue security arrangements for south Lebanon in accordance with the secret annex; neither would allow itself to be used as a staging ground for hostile activity against the other or a third state or permit movement through its territory by the armed forces of states hostile to the other; neither would intervene with the internal affairs of, or propagandize against, the other; both would together establish a Joint Liaison Committee aimed at developing "mutual relations" between the two states and maintain a liaison officer on the other's territory to carry out the functions of the committee. However, on the 8th, President Assad told Shultz that there would be no Syrian withdrawal based on the proposed accord. "It was about what we expected would happen," Shultz told the *Washington Post*.

Syria's refusal to leave Lebanon was devastating. One key amendment to the Israeli-Lebanese 17 May agreement—so called because it took until then to get Knesset approval in Israel—was that Israel was not obliged to bring its army home unless Syria did likewise. The provision became an issue of controversy among U.S. policymakers and raised serious doubts in the Pentagon regarding Israel's intentions and Secretary Shultz's instincts. Shultz had originally sanctioned the provision, believing it to be an empty formalism needed to win Knesset support. This Israeli withdrawal—which was the cornerstone of U.S. policy, and in which the United States had invested so much, so publicly—could be blocked by Assad, leaving the United States vulnerable to a leader who seemed to have every desire to embarrass the superpower.

Assad, in fact, showed no sign of withdrawing and added insult by making Habib officially persona non grata in Damascus. Moderate Arab reaction to the 17 May agreement gradually mirrored the initial Saudi response: There was little or none of the pressure the administration had anticipated. Israel soon made clear that it would make no unilateral movement. Lebanon's, and the region's, troubles seemed as distanced from solution as ever.

Those in the administration who had hoped to make Lebanon a demonstration of U.S. determination and influence as a superpower now feared that the failure of U.S. policy would instead appear to the world as a humiliating example of U.S. weakness. The NSC and top leadership at the State Department felt that the Soviet Union's close ties to and support of Syria raised the stakes in Lebanon to those of a full-blown superpower struggle.

Syria was the administration's new focal point. There were two reasons for this. One was that Syria's refusal to accept the 17 May agreement was keeping Israel in Lebanon—or at least so it seemed—and preventing the disengagement the United States had pledged to deliver. Another was that Syria was universally believed to be supporting Lebanon's Druze community in actions hostile to the government, making it difficult or impossible for the United States to succeed in encouraging Lebanon's political and military cohesion.

The situation in Lebanon was steadily disintegrating. The Shouf Mountains, strategic high ground overlooking the airport just southeast of Beirut, were historically Druze turf. Whereas the Israeli army, which still occupied the mountains, was able to control them, Lebanon's own government was not.

In early May, the LAF, backed by Gemayel's Phalange militia, attempted to extend the government's sway into the mountains but met stiff Druze and Palestinian resistance and eventually had to withdraw. Except for a brief war scare in late May, sparked by large Syrian maneuvers along Lebanon's border and a failed Syrian attack on an Israeli reconnaissance plane, relative quiet held throughout June and early July, when marines began patrolling Beirut with the LAF. But, in mid-July, an LAF patrol was ambushed by Druze militia and renewed fighting soon broke out in the Shouf Mountains. Then, on 22 July, the Druze shelled marine positions at the airport, wounding three marines and closing the airport.

The next day, Lebanese Druze leader Walid Jumblatt put a dire political gloss on the escalating violence by announcing the formation of the National Salvation Front, comprised of several Moslem groups and at least one prominent Maronite politician and backed by Syria. Its principal demands were a call for the rejection of the 17 May agreement and the creation of a new government based on a fresh census reflecting Lebanon's actual Moslem-dominated confessional balance. The combined militias of the front began to militarily engage the LAF and Gemayel's Phalange in southern and West Beirut and in the Shouf.

President Reagan's new special envoy to the Middle East was Deputy National Security Adviser Robert "Bud" McFarlane, who had been given the post shortly after Habib was rejected in Damascus. While the inconclusive debates continued in Washington, McFarlane spent most of the summer working—somewhat ironically—to prevent a partial Israeli withdrawal. Israel had decided that controlling the Shouf Mountains was too difficult and costly and wanted to withdraw the IDF south to the Awwali River. The United States, still pursuing a full Israeli disengagement, strenuously opposed any such partial withdrawal. For one thing, it opened up all the threatening high ground above the marines' vulnerable position at the airport, which the Lebanese government forces clearly could not control. For another, because Syria was believed to be furnishing the Druze in the Shouf with weapons and other aid, an Israeli withdrawal could easily be interpreted as the first unequivocal military success by Syria or Syrian-backed forces of the entire Lebanon engagement.

Israel was sympathetic to both concerns and put off its planned withdrawal three times. Matters in the Shouf did not improve, however; throughout August, the marines' positions at the airport took intermittent shellfire from Druze positions in the mountains. On 28 August, the marines returned fire for the first time, and the next day they used artillery to silence a Druze position in the hills after losing two men in a mortar attack. On Thursday, 1 September—the same day that the Soviet Union shot down KAL 007—Walid Jumblatt announced that the marines would henceforth be considered enemy forces. As Syrian hostility increased and Israeli withdrawal became imminent,

McFarlane proposed that the marines move from the airport to the Shouf and establish joint checkpoints with the LAF. He strongly advocated changing the balance of power in Lebanon through the application of U.S. force.

The Israelis moved out of the Shouf on 4 September. Christian Phalange forces moved into the mountains in their wake to engage the Druze, who were reportedly reinforced by Syrian and PLO forces, while the LAF occupied a key road junction closer to the airport. Shellfire from the mountains killed two marines and wounded two more. On the 5th, the Phalange were definitively defeated, forcing the LAF to attempt to defend the strategically situated town of Suq-al-Gharb to avoid conceding the Shouf above the airport to the Druze. The marines continued to take casualties and returned the fire. The attacks reflected how profoundly the U.S. position in Lebanon had changed since the MNF's introduction.

McFarlane continued to argue from Lebanon for an increased military role, against the strong protests of the marine commander in Beirut and the command authorities in Stuttgart, who saw neutrality as the best defense. At this time, administration insiders observed, McFarlane's role was comparable to that of Habib, in that, once again, the president's special envoy exercised extraordinary influence.

As a result of his persuasion, the military undertook a more active role. On 7 September, at Reagan's direction, F-14 fighters launched from the U.S. carriers off the coast of Beirut were used, for the first time, to locate hostile positions in the Shouf, and on the 8th, also for the first time, naval gunfire was used against them. The same day, President Gemayel asked the MNF nations to expand their forces and to use them more vigorously in support of his government. President Reagan responded: On the 12th, 2,000 more marines were moved to ships off Beirut. The Beirut marine commander was also authorized to call in strategic air strikes, and the White House determined, and informed the military, that the successful defense of Suq-al-Gharb was critical to the safety of the marines and, thus, covered under the formal rules of engagement limiting marine fire to self-defense (the State Department's Politico Military bureau had put in an extraordinary amount of time generating scholastic analyses to determine how far the United States could push discretionary military actions in the name of self-defense). McFarlane had pressed both measures on the marine commander against vigorous opposition. On the 19th, offshore destroyers fired on Druze in support of the LAF forces at Suq-al-Gharb. Finally, at the president's direction, the battleship *New Jersey,* which mounted sixteen-inch guns, arrived off Beirut on the 25th.

For those in the administration who advocated the use of military power, the U.S. escalation in September seemed to bear immediate fruit. On 26 September, McFarlane, in Damascus, negotiated a cease-fire with Assad; the fighting in the Shouf and the shelling of marines ceased. "When you look day by day at what Assad did when we began to rattle sabers, it's impressive," one senior White House official said. "The *New Jersey* wasn't even there, but the idea that it was coming led to a meeting that led to a cease-fire. It was, I think, clearly attributable to the potential application of force." Typical of issues relating to Lebanon, there were dissenting voices. Another high-ranking administration official argued that it was not U.S. firepower but the extent of the Lebanese strife that made Syria draw back. "[Assad's clients were getting out of hand,] and the Syrians felt that a chaotic situation was not one in which they could maximize their influence," he said. "At a very general level there was a coincidence of Syrian and U.S. interests: both were interested in achieving a cease-fire and trying to resolve things on a political basis, [even if their more specific goals were greatly at odds.]"

At that moment, there did realistically appear to be a certain congruence of United States and Syrian interests. As part of the negotiations on the cease-fire, Assad had agreed to recognize the legitimacy of the Gemayel government; for its part, the United States had promised to lean on Gemayel to make political concessions to his internal, and largely Syrian-backed, opposition. On the day the cease-fire was brokered, Gemayel set a 10 October date for the opening of a "National Dialogue" to include all of Lebanon's important factional leaders. For almost the first time, the United States began addressing Lebanon's internal political situation in the hope of easing tension through some rapprochement between the many militant politicians.

DISCUSSION QUESTIONS

1. *Why had the United States succeeded?*
2. *What could derail further progress?*
3. *Which of the parties had the most leverage to enforce the settlement? Which had the least?*
4. *How would you estimate the chances for further diplomatic breakthroughs at this point? What could cause the process to collapse?*
5. *In what ways did the U.S. role as third-party mediator in Lebanon compare to that in the Suez or Falklands/Malvinas cases? How had the decision to send U.S. marines to Lebanon elevated or diminished U.S. effectiveness and mediating capabilities? Had the dynamics of other key players in the negotiations acted to encourage or hinder a settlement?*

FURTHER READING ON THE LEBANON CRISIS

Ball, George. *Error and Betrayal in Lebanon: An Analysis of Israel's Invasion of Lebanon.* Washington, DC: Foundation for Middle East Peace, 1984.

Freidman, Thomas L. *From Beirut to Jerusalem*. New York: Farrar, Straus & Giroux, 1989.

Harkabi, Yehoshafat. *Israel's Fateful Decisions*, translated by Lenn Schramm. London: I. B. Tauris, 1988.

Scruton, Roger. *A Land Held Hostage: Lebanon and the West*. London: Claridge, 1987.

Sicker, Martin. *Israel's Quest for Security*. New York: Praeger, 1989.

7

DIPLOMACY DURING THE PERSIAN GULF WAR, 1990–1991

On 2 August 1990, the Iraqi army invaded Kuwait. The president of Iraq, Saddam Hussein, promoted himself to the rank of field marshal and declared that this invasion was executed at the invitation of Kuwaiti "revolutionaries" attempting to overthrow a "corrupt minority." Iraq's Revolutionary Command Council promised, in a subsequent statement, that the invading forces would be withdrawn "as soon as things settle and when the free provisional government asks us to do so. We hope that this will be a matter of a few days or a few weeks at the latest."[1] On 7 August, however, Hussein announced the annexation of Kuwait, ostensibly in response to the appeal of the "provisional" government that requested to rejoin "the mother homeland" through a "comprehensive and eternal merger."[2]

Seven months later, following the largest U.S. troop deployment since World War II, the most extensive aerial bombardment of any country since the Vietnam War, and a massive armored assault, Iraqi forces were ordered to cease fire and withdraw from Kuwait. Ironically, both Presidents Saddam and Bush declared victory. In the process, the army of Iraq had been decimated, the emir of Kuwait restored to sovereignty over the country, and the Saddam government compelled to comply with all pertinent U.N. resolutions condemning Iraq's aggression, including those requiring reparations for war damages and war crime trials for Iraqi leaders and officers accused of atrocities. Almost from day one, a wide variety of peacemakers attempted to find the common ground on which a negotiated settlement to the conflict could be constructed. In their perception, negotiation was a preferable alternative to

This chapter is an original case study developed especially for this book by Allan E. Goodman.

that of a more extensive war, in which Iraqi chemical weapons could conceivably be employed and into which countries such as Israel, which possessed nuclear weapons, might be drawn. Neither president appeared interested in negotiating.

As other cases in this volume indicate, war is commonplace in the Middle East. The region's bounty of historic-religious, natural, and geo-strategic resources have consistently proved to be a curse. The quest for secure and economical access to oil, in particular, provided a variety of external powers with incentive to carve a set of boundaries out of tribal patrimonies and vast deserts for purely selfish gains. With the exception of Egypt, the countries created by the outcome of the rivalry between the Ottoman and British empires did not contain a homogeneous mixture of citizens and the artificial boundaries of the new nations made little sense to the people and ethnic groups of the region. Throughout the region, there are lands—and under many of them, oil—coveted by others and subject to contradictory historical claims regarding the legitimate ownership of the territory. Many modern attempts to change borders by conflict can be rationalized as an extension of such historical disputes. The region has also had a disproportionate share of charismatic leaders, whose vision of their mission and suzerainty consistently reached beyond borders in an effort to unite all Arabs or all Moslems. Some believed that they had a special license from God to unite all followers of a particular religious sect as well as drive out nonbelievers, who they believed had imposed economic conditions that led to vast inequities in the distribution of regional wealth and power.

Saddam Hussein is one such leader. By the beginning of 1990, he had convinced many of his compatriots that they had a right to the lands and riches of Kuwait as well as a sacred duty to regain what had once been part of Iraqi territory. For nearly six months, Saddam tried to intimidate the leaders of Kuwait into sharing their oil wealth. Through the good offices of Saudi Arabia and the Organization of Petroleum Exporting Countries (OPEC), the two governments conducted an acrimonious but apparently fruitful series of negotiations over the Iraqi claim that Kuwait had undermined the former's economy by pumping too much oil (lowering the world wide price) and had tapped into the huge Rumaila oil field in such a way that it was actually extracting oil from beneath the territory of Iraq. During June and July, these negotiations produced an agreement (on 11 July) by the oil ministers of Kuwait, Qatar, Saudi Arabia, and the United Arab Emirates (UAE) to curb Kuwaiti and UAE oil production to a level of 1.5 million bpd (barrels per day) until the reference price of crude had been restored to $18 per barrel, a figure agreed on among OPEC nations in 1987. Iraq had argued that at the then-current price of $13.75, the nation would suffer a $3.5 billion current account deficit by the end of 1990.

However, Saddam Hussein was not satisfied with this agreement. On the anniversary (17 July) of the revolution that elevated him to power, he charged that Kuwaiti leaders had been using an oil weapon against Iraq for nearly a decade to weaken the Baath party and the nation in its war against Iran. Saddam claimed that this had been accomplished principally by "stealing" some $2.4 billion worth of oil from the Rumaila field and he threatened "cutting necks" rather than Iraq's "means of living" if "usurped rights" were not returned.[3]

Subsequently, another round of talks were undertaken, starting on 22 July, with a visit to Cairo by Foreign Minister Tariq Aziz. Until relatively late in the negotiations, Aziz and others continued to maintain that Iraq's dispute with Kuwait could and would be settled peacefully. Aziz consistently assured friendly Arab and Western governments that any observable troop movements or military buildup in southern Iraq were a normal part of planned exercises and scheduled rotations and should not be misconstrued as an effort to militarily intimidate Kuwait or as preparation for aggressive actions, should negotiations fail to produce an agreement satisfactory to Iraq. After meeting with Aziz, Egyptian president Hosni Mubarak said he was confident that Kuwait and Iraq would "arrive at a comfortable and calm, quiet solution."[4] On 24 July, Mubarak met personally with Saddam Hussein in Baghdad, where he received explicit guarantees that Iraq had no intention of attacking Kuwait, despite reports in the U.S. press that some 30,000 Iraqi troops (amounting to two armored divisions) had moved to the Kuwaiti border by 21 July. On 27 July, OPEC agreed to raise its reference price for crude oil to $21 per barrel and allow only a small total increase over 1989 in 1990 oil production.

Over the next three days, a massive Iraqi troop movement was under way so that by 30 July, some 100,000 troops protected by 300 tanks were now positioned on the Iraq-Kuwait border. In response, Jordan's King Hussein, PLO chairman Yasser Arafat, and Mubarak each communicated with Saddam Hussein and received individual assurances that an attack was not planned. These promises were conveyed to Washington.[5] Nevertheless, Iraqi rhetoric remained bellicose and another round of talks was scheduled for 31 July. Saddam Hussein stated that his representative was planning to attend these talks to "retain its [Iraq's] rights and not to hear talks about 'fraternity and solidarity' which yield nothing."[6] Iraqi demands, at this point, according to reports appearing in the *International Herald Tribune* (1 August 1990), included the following:

- $10 billion in aid from Kuwait and other wealthy Arab countries to assist in recovering from the war with Iran;
- $2.4 billion in compensation from Kuwait for the "stolen" oil referred to previously;
- the cancellation of $10 billion of its external debt;

- renunciation by Kuwait of any claim over the Rumaila oil field; and
- a long-term lease on two long-coveted islands that Hussein felt would secure Iraq's access to the Gulf.

These talks collapsed after two hours, but the region's leaders, who had been in contact with Saddam, were still not convinced that war was imminent.

REACHING THE DECISION TO NEGOTIATE

While the U.S. government watched these events with increasing attention and then concern, the Bush administration apparently did not suspect the magnitude of Iraqi aspirations or their inclination to use force. Just nine days before the invasion, the U.S. ambassador to Iraq, April Glaspie, met Saddam Hussein and, according to Iraqi press reports, indicated that the Bush administration had "no opinion on the Arab-Arab conflicts, like your border disagreement with Kuwait."[7] Apparently, Saddam appraised the statement as a message of U.S. disinterest and viewed the dialogue as a green light to invade Kuwait. In dispute of what she termed Iraqi "fabrication" and "disinformation" in regard to her message, Glaspie claimed that Saddam chose to exploit the rushed circumstances of their contact by apparently ignoring the first half of her statement, in which she emphasized the U.S. commitment to peaceful and nonaggressive settlement of regional disputes. She also "told him orally we would defend our vital interests, we would support our friends in the Gulf, we would defend their sovereignty and integrity."[8] However, another official statement, on 24 July, may also have caught Saddam's attention and reinforced his perception of U.S. indifference. The spokesperson for the Department of State noted, in commenting on the dispatch of six navy ships to the Gulf for exercises with the naval forces of the UAE, that "we do not have any defense treaties with Kuwait, and there are no special defense or security commitments to Kuwait."[9]

But for most of the 1980s, relations between Washington and Baghdad had been cordial enough to mislead any leader into thinking that the United States was unlikely to actively oppose an effort to settle some ancient score. In 1984, full diplomatic relations with Iraq had been restored and the country had been removed from the list of those suspected of sponsoring terrorism. In 1987, the United States accepted Iraq's apology for mistakenly firing an Exocet missile at the frigate *USS Stark,* killing thirty-seven U.S. sailors. In 1988, the Reagan administration blocked a congressional effort to impose sanctions against Iraq for the use of poison gas against the Kurds, and between 1985 and 1990 the U.S. Department of Commerce authorized the export of a wide range of material to Iraq, that was directly relevant to the country's development of ballistic missiles as well as chemical and nuclear weapons. In fact, the department promoted high-tech exports to Iraq, between 1985 and 1990, approving 771 licenses to export $1.5 worth of computers, chemicals, and communications equipment, all with the potential to serve military as well as civilian objectives. Ironically, the Iraqi military command-and-control system, which was targeted by U.S. planes in 1991, was purchased from the United States in 1989. The *Washington Post* reported that, as of 1990, nearly 500 export licenses worth about three-quarters of a billion dollars had been approved with another 160 under review on the eve of the invasion. Loans to Iraq to finance these and other massive agricultural imports had reached the $1 billion mark by this time and overall trade with the United States had increased to $3.6 billion. Furthermore, between 1983 and 1989, the United States had purchased more than $5.5 billion in Iraqi oil.[10]

Nevertheless, Saddam Hussein probably had some reasons to speculate that his militant actions might eventually run the risk of generating an external response. Historically, U.S. actions, if not their verbal communications, had consistently demonstrated a tendency toward U.S. intervention in the disputes of the Gulf region. Regional stability is perceived as fundamental to the achievement of key U.S. goals in the Middle East, such as the protection of Israel, the prevention of expanded Soviet influence, and the security of the vital oil exports. As recently as 1987, during the Iran-Iraq War, the United States reaffirmed its intention to safeguard the flow of oil in the Gulf by agreeing to re-flag eleven Kuwaiti tankers with U.S. flags and providing U.S. naval escorts in order to insure safe passage.

Consequently, Saddam planned to deter an immediate U.S. response to the Iraqi invasion of Kuwait by combining this aggressive act with outrageous threats and intimations of Arab alliances. When his forces invaded Kuwait, he protected his hostile territorial gains by holding the conquered nation hostage and threatening to "turn Kuwait into a graveyard"[11] if the United States or any other foreign power intervened. Saddam also attempted to rally the support of other Arab nations by emphasizing the disparity of Kuwaiti wealth and Iraqi poverty and by highlighting ancient Iraqi claims to the Kuwaiti territory.

The immediate U.S. response to Saddam's actions was to order naval forces to the Gulf, conduct urgent consultations with its Arab allies, and lobby with the Soviet Union for a strong U.N. condemnation of Iraqi aggression. On 2 August, the Security Council unanimously adopted Resolution 660, which condemned the invasion of Kuwait, demanded Iraq's immediate and unconditional withdrawal, and called for the beginning of negotiations between Iraq and Kuwait. Fearing an Iraqi advance across their borders, the Saudi government appealed to the United States for defense. In response to the Saudi invitation, the United States dispatched advance elements of the army and marines to prevent an invasion of that country. In addition, British, French, and Soviet naval vessels were ordered to head to the Gulf on a defensive mission. Neighboring countries in the Gulf region reacted quickly to the Iraqi aggression, as Egypt pledged to send troops to assist in the defense of Saudi Arabia and the Saudis and the Turks shut down the oil pipelines used by Iraq. Eventually this troop presence would grow to some 540,000 U.S. and 205,000 Allied troops; more than 115 ships and 2,790 aircraft would also become involved in operations Desert Shield and Desert Storm.

By 11 August, two more U.N. Security Council resolutions had been passed. Resolution 661 imposed a trade and financial embargo on Iraq and called for the restoration of the legitimate government of Kuwait. Resolution 662 declared that Iraq's annexation of Kuwait (announced on 8 August) was null and void.

In response, Saddam Hussein detained thousands of foreign workers and their families and offered a peace plan for the region that involved both the Iraqi withdrawal from Kuwait and, among other things, Israel's withdrawal from the occupied territories on the West Bank of the Jordan River and the Gaza Strip. This plan was almost as shocking as the invasion itself because until that moment the Iraqi invasion appeared solely motivated by Saddam's greed for money and territory and his long-standing grievances against the monarchy of Kuwait. In retrospect, however, analysts in Washington observed a growing number of statements made by Saddam in early 1990 that were directed against Israel and advocating a holy war to regain Jerusalem for the Arabs and a homeland for the Palestinians. Clearly such linkage made sense for Saddam if he hoped to garner support among Arab nations, and in so doing deny the United States an adequate regional consensus to compel an Iraqi withdrawal. But the linkage Saddam Hussein was creating between his actions and the need for a comprehensive discussion of the causes for conflict and instability throughout the region also convinced some analysts in Washington, as well as in Europe and the Arab world, that negotiations were both possible and desirable at this point. Negotiating would presumably compel the United States and other powers to ultimately tackle the root problems (i.e., the Arab-Israeli-Palestinian disputes and hatreds, and the external powers that reinforced and fueled them) that lay at the source of the region's seemingly endless tendency toward war.

DISCUSSION QUESTIONS

1. *What do you think Saddam Hussein's objectives are at this early point in the conflict? Has he been misled by U.S. signals about Arab-Arab disputes? What is his strategy?*

2. *What indicators would you advise President Bush to look for to determine if Saddam is serious about wanting to seek a negotiated settlement of the conflict? Does Bush want to negotiate?*

3. *To which countries might President Bush appeal to assist in opening a dialogue with Saddam? What other countries might want to try to create such a dialogue with Iraq regardless of Washington's desires? What would be their motivations?*
4. *What leverage does the United States have over Iraq at this point? Do any other countries have additional leverage?*
5. *What are the costs of indicating or signalling a willingness to seek negotiations at this point? Over the longer term?*
6. *What do you think Saddam Hussein expects President Bush to do?*

GETTING TO THE TABLE

Between 11 and 20 August, and despite a flurry of public and private Arab diplomacy to initiate negotiations that would avoid any further U.S. military buildup, Saddam Hussein did not facilitate the establishment of U.S.-Iraqi talks or any basis or in any fora. Quite the contrary. In fact, on 15 August, Saddam offered peace to its former enemy Iran. Then, on 16-17 August, the Iraqi government instructed all foreign workers and their families to report to designated locations and threatened to confine some of them as guests at sensitive and strategic military installations. Evidently, exploitation of these civilians as human "shields" incensed U.S. and European leaders, as did the increasingly bellicose rhetoric of Saddam Hussein. Consequently, on 22 August, President Bush and Prime Minister Margaret Thatcher of Great Britain jointly rejected Saddam's call for talks. A day later, the president called up the reserves. By 25 August, the U.N. Security Council passed a resolution (665) calling on member states with warships in the region to enforce sanctions by boarding and inspecting the cargoes of any vessel thought to be aiding Iraq. In early September, moreover, Presidents Bush and Gorbachev at a mini-summit in Helsinki reaffirmed their solidarity against Iraq. Eventually, seven more Security Council resolutions would be passed in the hope that such political pressure, coupled to the effects of the economic sanctions, would force Saddam Hussein to seek a basis on which to withdraw from Kuwait without losing face or fighting a major war with the growing number of allied forces currently establishing a significant military presence in the Gulf.

As an overwhelming international consensus was mounting in support of the liberation of Kuwait and against the Iraqi aggression, Saddam Hussein appeared to be adamantly consolidating and hardening his position. On 28 August, Iraq declared Kuwait to be its nineteenth province. And by mid-September, Saddam, along with the supreme religious leader of Iran, the Ayatollah Ali Khamenei, had called for a holy war against Israel and all foreign forces opposing Iraq. Subsequently, attitudes became increasingly inflexible on both sides.

From this point on, the diplomats realized the need to revise U.S. objectives and influence Iraqi behavior. The central issue had become how to make Saddam Hussein realize that he would pay a very heavy price for remaining in Kuwait—it had become clear that he would not be forced out by current words or deeds.

Numerous efforts were made by European and Arab leaders to deliver this message to Saddam Hussein and at the same time propose formulas by which an Iraqi withdrawal from Kuwait would lead to broader-scope negotiations over the future of the Middle East. Arab experts in Washington and Europe consistently warned of the long-term consequences of a war with Iraq to the stability of the region.[12] These warnings added to the pressure on President Bush to devote as much attention to the diplomatic as to the military options before him. Even top U.S. military commanders, such as General Norman Schwarzkopf, were speaking publicly during this period about finding "alternatives to destroying Saddam Hussein and his regime."[13]

Nothing was to come of these efforts, however, until President Bush ordered U.S. troop strength increased in the Gulf by some 150,000 soldiers, to a total of 380,000. Speaking at a press conference on 8 November, the president said the move—the largest deployment of U.S. forces since the Vietnam War—was designed to "insure that the coalition has an adequate offensive military option should that be necessary." Bush reiterated his demand that "Saddam Hussein should fully without condition comply to the U.N. resolutions. And if this movement of force is what convinces him, so much the better."[14] The next day, Secretary of Defense Dick Cheney confirmed the extent of U.S. military commitment in the region by announcing that U.S. troops in and headed for the Gulf would not be rotated until the crisis was over. Following this announcement, Secretary of State James Baker visited key members of the coalition and reported that solid agreement existed among the powers in their refusal to accept partial solutions or a limited Iraqi withdrawal and that there was strong endorsement by the leaders of the coalition for the president's decision to increase U.S. troop strength and develop a credible military option.

No one can be certain of the provocation or rationale behind Saddam Hussein's promise, which shortly followed these events on 18 November, to free some of the captive Iraqi foreign "guests" immediately and the rest by 25 December. However, this magnanimous gesture was not followed by additional indications of Saddam's willingness to discuss full compliance with the existing U.N. resolutions. And on 29 November, the U.N. Security Council passed Resolution 678, which authorized member states "to use all necessary means" to force Iraq out of Kuwait if it did not withdraw voluntarily by 15 January 1991.

As a concession to international pressure, President Bush proposed that Baker and Aziz meet in Washington for talks prior to the deadline. This proposal was an essential ingredient in the procurement of international approval for the U.N. resolution. The United States suggested the week of 10 December.

There were reasons to hope at this point that Saddam Hussein was, in fact, interested in such a dialogue. In a two-hour interview with Peter Jennings of ABC News two weeks earlier, Saddam struck the first conciliatory posture of the crisis and indicated that he was, indeed, prepared to negotiate with Washington. The Iraqi leader said he had "been ready all along." Saddam was quick to point out, however, that he would not entertain the idea of pulling his troops out of Kuwait before such talks began, rejecting any and all "preconditions."[15] On 2 December, Saddam formally accepted Bush's offer and attempted to impose some linkages of his own. Iraq's interpretation of the nature of an agenda for the talks is captured in the following excerpt from the statement issued by the Revolutionary Command Council in response to President Bush's proposal.

We learned about a statement made by Bush yesterday as it was disseminated by news agencies. In his statement, he proposes inviting the Iraqi Foreign Minister to Washington for a meeting with him, and sending his Secretary of State to Baghdad to meet leader President Saddam Hussein. . . .

We believe that human interaction, for it to be sincere, must be based on justice and equality eliminating all forms of tyranny, political intransigence, threats, social oppression and exploitation. On the debris of the era of oppression and dictation practiced by the superpowers, foremost of which is the United States, we must build a new form of democratic relations among the peoples of the world. . . .

We believe that, in order to accomplish cooperation, it should be the result of deep interaction among nations and peoples. And in order to achieve cooperation, dialogue should be preferred over any other method. Our announcements on this have been frequent.

The enemy of God, the arrogant President of the United States, George Bush, always rejected dialogue, voicing his contempt of the Arabs and Muslims, and all those who believe in God and human values in the world.

Despite the fact that Bush's call for the meeting came after he had mobilized all the criminal forces on the holy places of the Arabs and Muslims, after he had issued unjust resolutions through the so-called Security Council against the people of Iraq and despite the arrogant language he used in his call . . . and in harmony with our principles and the ethics and morals that Almighty God called on us to abide by, we accept the idea of the invitation and the meeting.

When we receive the invitations officially, those concerned in Iraq and those concerned in the United States will agree on the timing and practical arrangements of the exchange of visits to suit both sides.

Because the call for the meeting contains an idea whose purposes are not clear enough—namely, the U.S. President's invitation to several countries' ambassadors to attend the meeting between himself and the Iraqi Foreign Minister, we will inquire from the American side about this idea and the reasons for it.

If the American side believes that it is necessary, Iraq, for its part, will call on representatives of countries and parties that are connected with unresolved disputes and issues to attend the meetings between Iraq and the U.S. Administration, whether in Washington or Baghdad. This will take place after consultations with the concerned parties on the basis of reciprocity.

In any case, our efforts will continue, as always, to hold an in-depth, serious dialogue, not formal meetings as sought by the American President to use as a pretext for American public opinion, the U.S. Congress, world public opinion and the international community to achieve objectives that he planned in the first place.

Iraq will continue to follow up and expand any room for dialogue instead of using threats and warnings. The principles of leader President Saddam Hussein's initiative of August 12, 1990, will be our guide in any serious dialogue.

Palestine and the other occupied Arab territories will remain before our eyes and at the forefront of the issues that we will discuss in any dialogue.[16]

DISCUSSION QUESTIONS

1. *In authorizing the member states participating in Operation Desert Shield "to use all necessary means" to restore peace and security to the Gulf, the United Nations Security Council has acknowledged that only the use of force may now drive Iraq out of Kuwait. Nevertheless, President Bush is under considerable pressure from Congress to refrain from exercising this option, and he has invited the Iraqi foreign minister to hold discussions in Washington during the week of 10 December.*

   The president has asked you to help prepare him for those discussions. Specifically, the president would like your assessment of the following:

- *the impact of sanctions and this latest U.N. resolution on the outlook and goals of Saddam Hussein and those who influence him;*
- *how the discussions with the Iraqi foreign minister could possibly lead to negotiations;*
- *the strategy and tactics the United States should be prepared to follow in such negotiations; and*
- *whether there are any alternatives to war if the discussions next week prove fruitless.*

2. *In dealing with this last question, the president has mentioned that Article 33 of the U.N. Charter offers a good inventory of diplomatic and other tools for conflict resolution. This article provides that "the parties to a dispute, the continuation of which is likely to endanger the maintenance of international peace and security, shall, first of all, seek a solution by negotiation, enquiry, mediation, conciliation, arbitration, judicial settlement, resort to regional agencies or arrangements, or other peaceful means of their own choice."*

Short of war, does the United Nations have any leverage that would compel Iraq to respond positively to any of these means of settling the crisis in the Gulf?

BREAKING THE DEADLOCK

Despite the indicators and rhetoric in early December suggesting that the Iraqi leadership was indeed prepared to enter into a dialogue with Washington to achieve an end to the conflict, such talks were never held. Iraq refused to accept the date for the Baker-Aziz meeting in Washington, proposed by President Bush. Saddam Hussein pushed instead for a postponement of the meeting, suggesting that a meeting between Secretary Baker and Saddam be held in Baghdad on 12 January, only a few days before the deadline contained in the U.N. resolution, authorizing the use of force if Iraq showed no signs of willingness to comply with U.N. resolutions. President Bush argued that the date would not give the negotiators sufficient time to work out terms for the Iraqi withdrawal if Saddam were, in fact, legitimately interested in taking this step. Nevertheless, there were also some encouraging developments. On 6 December, Saddam announced the release of all foreign "guests"/hostages. And as late as 18 December, when it appeared that no agreement on a date for the talks was likely to be reached, President Bush still predicted there was a chance that Saddam Hussein would withdraw from Kuwait. As he told a *Time* magazine interviewer, "My gut says he will get out of there."[17] The president set a deadline of 3 January for Iraq to furnish a date for a Baker-Aziz meeting, prior to the 12 January.

On that day, the Iraqis finally agreed to talks in Geneva on 9 January. Speaking for the Iraqi leadership, Aziz said in a statement broadcast on Baghdad radio:

> Iraq has always stressed and would like to stress now its constant attitude, namely that it does not fear pressure and does not determine its attitude under threats and intimidation. Despite this bad way used by the American Administration, Iraq out of respect to world public opinion and to recognized norms of dealing between nations and not out of appreciation to the position taken by the American Administration and its bad attitude, has responded positively to the American proposal.[18]

Although this particular statement hardly suggested that the talks would be fruitful, Aziz gave a number of interviews on the eve of the talks that suggested that "Iraq is open to genuine, sincere, serious intention to make peace in the whole region of the Middle East, we are ready to reciprocate."[19]

The talks lasted for more than six hours, giving rise initially to hopes that a breakthrough was conceivable. Secretary of State Baker characterized the talks as "serious" and the tone "good." "We weren't pounding the table and shouting at each other; it was a very reasoned and I think responsible discussion by two diplomats who really would like to find a peaceful and political solution to this problem. But . . . I did not detect flexibility in the position of Iraq."[20] In his press conference after the talks, Aziz agreed with Secretary Baker's characterization and also noted that there remained "grave, or big differences." When asked if he now considered war with the United States to be inevitable, Aziz responded, "That is up to the American administration to decide. I told Mr. Baker that we are prepared for all expectations . . . Iraq will defend itself in a very bold manner. We are a courageous nation, and we deeply feel that we have been treated unjustly."[21]

According to those who were in the Oval Office as Secretary Baker called in his report on the meeting, President Bush took the news of the deadlock in Geneva very hard.

> The President excused himself to take the call and was gone for about eight minutes. When he came back, our conversation stopped. The President's whole demeanor had changed. He was somber and grim. You could see it all over his face. He looked at us and said two words: "No progress." I felt it was a defining moment. He was a different man.[22]

A few days later, on 13 January, U.N. secretary-general Xavier Perez de Cuellar had a similar reaction when he finished his meeting with Saddam

Hussein. The secretary-general had hoped to arrange some further talks to offset the deadline for using force. He returned to New York reporting that as far as diplomacy was concerned, the situation was "hopeless." "At 3 A.M. (Iraq time) on 17 January, Operation Desert Shield became Desert Storm."

Within days of the initiation of the air war against Iraq, diplomats again sought a means of salvation from the realities of war. Some did so representing countries like Algeria and India that have traditionally played the role of peacemaker between the United States and hostile Arab countries. Others did so in the service of a country like Iran, which was seeking to reassert its position as a regional power and to assure that, if a compromise were to be reached, Iranian interests would be protected if not enhanced. And still others represented countries like the Soviet Union, Pakistan, and Yugoslavia (chair of the nonaligned nations movement), whose leaders appeared motivated by concern that U.S. goals and military actions would expand the scope of the war well beyond original expectations and limitations of the U.N. resolution authorizing force. To all of these peacemakers, the vivid images associated with the thousands of tons of explosives dropped by U.S. and allied forces on Iraq and Iraqi forces in Kuwait during the first days of the air war—rather than the Iraqi invasion and rape of Kuwait—were outrageous. They became convinced that an end to the war and the preservation of a viable Iraqi government were of cardinal importance to international relations and regional stability.

President Bush and his coalition partners did not share the outlook of the would-be peacemakers. The U.S., British, French, Saudi, and Egyptian leadership steadfastly maintained that the future of the international system, and the hope for a "new order" in the Middle East in particular, depended on punishing this instance of aggression and making it impossible for Saddam Hussein to provoke a war with any of his neighbors again. Indeed, the more the war was prosecuted and the more bellicose Saddam Hussein's rhetoric became, the more U.S. and allied leaders appeared convinced that the region and the world would only be safe if Iraq complied with all U.N. resolutions—including those calling for Saddam to be held accountable for committing war crimes. At several points during the period of conflict, moreover, president Bush appealed to the people of Iraq to overthrow Saddam so that their nation and the entire region could be restored to peace. At no point did the president appear to signal the least bit of interest in arranging a compromise with Saddam Hussein, and he focused all of his personal diplomacy on maintaining the international coalition against Iraq.

If at this point Saddam Hussein had a plan in mind to end the war by a negotiated settlement, it probably looked like this:

- Withstand Allied bombing heroically (accomplished), move the best aircraft to safe haven in Iran (accomplished), engage Allied armored forces on the ground to show Arab bravery (accomplished at Kafji), declare victory and withdraw some forces from Kuwait so as to remain a hero and in power.

• Negotiate (for such "side effects" as splitting the Allied coalition and buying time to resupply forces in southern Iraq and northern Kuwait) over the terms and rate of withdrawal from Kuwait.

On 15 February, Iraq's Revolutionary Command Council indeed did propose that Iraqi forces voluntarily withdraw from Kuwait if the Allied forces pulled out of the Gulf region and Israel ended its occupation of the West Bank. The White House immediately rejected this "offer," reiterating the demands that Iraq comply with all U.N. resolutions and that Iraqi military withdrawal from Kuwait must be "complete and unconditional" and indicated by "concrete actions on the ground." [23] In reply, Iraq's U.N. representative said (on 16 February) that the proposal did not contain "conditions" but "legitimate issues" to be addressed.[24] Saddam Hussein, however, in a radio address on 18 February, rejected all demands that Iraqi forces withdraw from Kuwait unconditionally and declared that "our people and armed forces are determined to continue the struggle."[25] Saddam was to maintain this position almost to the end of the war.

By far the most significant and promising diplomacy was that conducted by the Soviet Union. The Soviet initiative grew out of ideas developed during a meeting in Washington at the end of January between Secretary of State Baker and the new Soviet foreign minister, Aleksandr Bessmertnykh. But the more Iraq was bombed, the less Saddam Hussein seemed willing to concede to end the war. At this point in time, the Iraqi leader probably thought that his forces had a better chance of defeating the United States on the ground—or inflicting enough casualties to compel Washington to soften its demands or even accept the Soviet peace plan—than by continuing to withstand an air war, against which Iraqi weapons proved useless. Thus Saddam was intent on stalling because he believed the probability of Iraqi victory increased as the war continued and evolved. So as the diplomats labored feverishly, in attempting to create what was to be the last chance for Presidents Bush and Saddam to adopt a face-saving way for both the United States and Iraq to avoid fighting a ground war, Saddam Hussein repeatedly stonewalled. The sequence of events was as follows.

1. **The Baker-Bessmertnykh "plan" is introduced on 29 January 1991.**

Description:

The war could end if Iraq "would make an unequivocal commitment" to leave Kuwait and take "immediate concrete steps" to do so.

Developments:

Disavowed by White House spokesperson shortly after it was released by the State Department in communiqué form. Later considered to be the essence of the proposal made by President Gorbachev in his meeting with Iraqi foreign minister Aziz in Moscow on 18 February. (See #3 of this list.)

2. The Hashemi Rafsanjani plan is introduced on 4 February 1991.

Description:

An unpublished seven-point proposal developed by Iranian president Rafsanjani that included a pledge by Iran to "do everything in its power" to get the United States and Allied forces out of the region in return for Iraqi withdrawal from Kuwait and their replacement by "Islamic forces."[26]

Developments:

The Iraqi deputy prime minister, Saddoun Hammadi, returning from Tehran on 9-10 February, ruled out a withdrawal from Kuwait (as suggested by Iran) and indicated in a two-hour press conference that Iraq was determined to continue to fight. "We have told Iran that what is taking place is unrelated to Kuwait. The question now is American aggression."[27] Hammadi advocated forming an Arab-Moslem united front against the Allied coalition and for severing diplomatic relations with the United States and other countries supporting the war in the Gulf.

3. The Gorbachev peace plan, is introduced between 4 and 23 February 1991.

Description:

After a cease-fire goes into effect, Iraq would "withdraw immediately and unconditionally all its forces from Kuwait" within a twenty-one-day period and under U.N. supervision. Once this withdrawal was complete, all U.N. resolutions sanctioning Iraq "will cease to operate." All prisoners of war would be repatriated within three days of the start of the cease-fire.

Developments:

- The Communist party of the Soviet Union issued an urgent "instruction" (on 4 February) to the Soviet president, which resulted in a direct appeal by Mikhail Gorbachev (9 February) to Saddam Hussein "to analyze again what is at stake for his country, to display realism which would make it possible to take the path of a reliable and just peaceful settlement." Gorbachev also expressed concern that the pace of war would create "a threat of going beyond the mandate" of the U.N. resolutions or widen the war to an Arab-Israeli conflict.[28]

- Hussein and Soviet special envoy Yevgeny M. Primakov met in Baghdad on 12 February. Hussein "affirmed . . . [that] Iraq has always called for tackling the situation in the region . . . through dialogue and political and peaceful means." Hussein also indicated that he would continue to resist U.S., Zionist, and other aggression.[29]

- Iraqi foreign minister Aziz met with President Gorbachev on 18 February and carried the terms of his proposal back to Baghdad.

- In response to Soviet efforts, the White House spokesperson indicated on 18 February that the U.S. position remained unchanged: Iraq must unconditionally withdraw from Kuwait. On 19 February, President Bush issued a statement that the Soviet plan "falls well short of what would be required" for the United States to stop the war and declared "there are no negotiations."[30]

- Iranian foreign minister Ali Akbar Velayati, at a 19 February press conference in Bonn, said that Tariq Aziz (who stopped over in Tehran en route from Moscow) convinced him that Iraq was "ready to withdraw from Kuwait unconditionally."[31]

- On the evening of 21 February, a spokesperson for President Gorbachev announced that on the basis of meetings with Tariq Aziz, "the two parties came to the conclusion that it is possible to find a way out of the military conflict."

- White House and other U.S. officials, however, consistently maintained that the proposal imposed conditions that were unacceptable to the United States and the coalition partners and that "no negotiation [was] under way."[32] President Bush personally rejected the Soviet plan as a basis for ending the conflict in a Rose Garden press conference on 22 February and gave Saddam Hussein until noon, 23 February, to agree to withdraw unconditionally from Kuwait.

- The Iraqi information minister responded to Bush later in the day by calling him "an enemy of God" and then rejecting what was termed "Bush's shameful ultimatum."[33]

- President Gorbachev's special envoy and the foreign minister conducted additional negotiations with Tariq Aziz in Moscow aimed at "adjusting" the Soviet proposal to meet Washington's objections. A Gorbachev spokesperson later indicated in a statement issued late on 22 February that the agreement had been "toughened" and that a reply was now awaited from

Baghdad. On 23 February, Tariq Aziz issued a statement from Moscow that said that "the Iraqi Government fully endorses this plan and fully supports it."[34] Washington did not.

- The 23 February noon deadline passed without a breakthrough. The White House issued a statement of regret, indicating that "military action continues on schedule and according to plan."[35] In a radio address broadcast by CNN on 23 February, Saddam Hussein expressed continued defiance and promised to turn Kuwait into "a crater of death."

The ground war portion of Operation Desert Storm began shortly afterward. Allied forces pushed deep into Kuwait and Iraq, encountering little resistance, and eventually destroyed much of Iraq's army. At approximately 6 P.M. EST, on 25 February, Radio Baghdad announced that orders had been issued "to our armed forces to withdraw in an organized manner to the positions held prior to August 1, 1990. This is regarded as a practical compliance with Resolution 660." The statement indicated that the Iraqi foreign minister was also in touch with President Gorbachev "requesting him to exert efforts at the Security Council to achieve a cease-fire and put an end to the criminal behavior of the United States and its allies and collaborators."[36] The White House said that it could not confirm that such a withdrawal was taking place and that such action, as announced, would not constitute compliance with all relevant U.N. resolutions. As a result, spokesperson Marlin Fitzwater declared, "The war goes on."[37]

DISCUSSION QUESTIONS

1. *Short of continuing and widening the war at this point, does the multinational coalition have any leverage that would now require Iraq to respond positively to any of these proposals for settling the crisis in the Gulf?*
2. *What would be the most likely scenario in your judgment to lead to a renewal of talks between Iraq and the coalition after 25 February?*
3. *Would your assessment of the prospects for a diplomatic solution to the conflict at this point have changed if Saddam Hussein were to have been replaced by a military junta?*
4. *What are the lessons of this episode regarding the role of force and diplomacy in establishing a "new world order"?*
5. *How were the foreign and domestic circumstances of the U.S.-Iraqi negotiation efforts distinct from those in the previous cases? To what degree could the failure to construct an agreement between the parties be attributed to these differences in conditions? What part did the end of the cold war play in these events?*

6. *How did the U.S. role in the negotiations to free Kuwait resemble or differ from that in the World War I or Vietnam cases? Would further talks have been productive? Did a viable alternative to force exist at the time? How did the U.N. role compare to that in the Suez crisis?*

NOTES

1. As reported by *New York Times*, 3 August 1990, p. A-8.

2. As reported by *New York Times*, 3 August 1990, p. A-10.

3. As reported in *New York Times*, 18 July 1990, p. D-1.

4. As reported by *Washington Post*, 24 July 1990, p. 18.

5. For details, see Thomas L. Friedman and Patrick E. Tyler, "From the First, U.S. Resolve to Fight," *New York Times*, 3 March 1991, p. 18.

6. As reported by *Los Angeles Times*, 3 August 1990, p. 12.

7. Ambassador April Glaspie, quoted in Lionel Barber, "How Washington Slid Away from Conciliation," *Financial Times*, 18 January 1991.

8. According to Glaspie's later congressional testimony, Hussein's incentive to strike Kuwait emanated solely from his own stupidity and miscalculations rather than from her statements. She observed that, unfortunately, U.S. policymakers did not recognize the depth of the communication gap: "Like every other government, we did not understand that he [Hussein] would be impervious to logic and diplomacy." *New York Times*, 21 March 1991.

9. Judith Miller and Laurie Mylroie, *Saddam Hussein and the Crisis in the Gulf* (New York: Random House for Times Books, 1990), p. 18.

10. *Ibid.,* p. 150.

11. As reported by *New York Times*, 3 August 1990, p. A-8.

12. See, for example, the forecasts contained in Michael Hudson and Bernard Picchi, *Crisis in the Persian Gulf: Political Causes and Oil Market Effects* (New York: Salomon Brothers Stock Research/Oils, October 1990).

13. Quoted in Peter Riddell, "US Commander in Gulf Urges Cautious Line," *Financial Times*, Weekend, 3-4 November 1990.

14. As reported by *New York Times*, 9 November 1990, p. 1.

15. Remarks reported in Philip Shendon, "Hussein Offering to Talk with US," *New York Times*, 16 November 1990, p. 14.

16. As reported by *New York Times*, 2 December 1990, p. A-18.

17. Reported in Friedman and Tyler, "From the First, U.S. Resolve to Fight," p. 18.

18. Excerpt from "Text of Report by Iraq Accepting US Plan," as reported in *New York Times*, 5 January 1991, p. 5.

19. Quoted in *New York Times*, 9 January 1991, p. A-6.

20. From Secretary Baker's press conference in Geneva as reported by *New York Times*, 10 January 1991, p. A-15.

21. As reported by *New York Times*, 10 January 1991, p. A-15.

22. Member of Congress Mel Levine, quoted in Friedman and Tyler, "From the First, U.S. Resolve to Fight," p. 18.

23. As reported by *Boston Globe*, 15 February 1991, p. 1.

24. As reported by *New York Times*, 16 February 1991, p. 5.

25. As reported by *Los Angeles Times*, 22 February 1991, p. 8.

26. As reported by *New York Times*, 10 February 1991, p. 19.

27. As reported by *New York Times*, 10 February 1991, citing the Kuwaiti newspaper *Sawt Al-Kuwait*, p. 19.

28. As reported by *New York Times*, 10 February 1991, p. 19.

29. As reported by *New York Times*, 13 February 1991, p. 14.

30. As reported by *New York Times*, 20 February 1991, p. A-1.

31. As reported by *New York Times*, 20 February 1991, p. A-12.

32. As reported by *New York Times*, 22 February 1991, p. A-7.

33. As reported by *New York Times*, 23 February 1991, p. 26.

34. As reported by *New York Times*, 24 February 1991, p. 19.

35. As reported by *USA Today*, 25 February 1991, p. 6A.

36. As reported by *New York Times*, 26 February 1991, p. 1.

37. As reported by *Boston Globe*, 26 February 1991, p. 3.

FURTHER READING ON THE MIDDLE EAST

Fromkin, David. *A Peace to End All Peace: Creating the Modern Middle East, 1914-1922.* New York: Henry Holt & Co., 1989.

Hameed, Mazher A. *Arabia Imperiled: The Security Imperative of the Arab Gulf States.* Washington, DC: Middle East Assessments Group, 1986.

Hudson, Michael C., and Bernard J. Picchi. *Crisis in the Persian Gulf: Political Causes and Oil Market Effects.* New York: Salomon Brothers Stock Research/Oils, October 1990.

Kipper, Judith, and Harold H. Saunders, eds. *The Middle East in Global Perspective.* Boulder, CO: Westview Press, 1991.

Khadduri, Majid. *The Gulf War: The Origins and Implications of the Iran-Iraq Conflict.* New York: Oxford University Press, 1988.

al-Khalil, Samir. *Republic of Fear: The Politics of Modern Iraq.* Los Angeles and Berkeley: University of California Press, 1989.

Marr, Phebe. *The Modern History of Iraq.* Boulder, CO: Westview Press, 1991.

Miller, Judith, and Laurie Mylroie, *Saddam Hussein and the Crisis in the Gulf.* New York: Random House for Times Books, 1990.

Newsom, David D., ed. *The Diplomatic Record 1990-1991.* Boulder, CO: Westview Press, 1991.

Safran, Nadav. *Saudi Arabia: The Ceaseless Quest for Security*. Cambridge, MA: Harvard University Press, 1985.

Tripp, Charles. *Iran and Iraq at War*. Boulder, CO: Westview Press, 1991.

Yergin, Daniel. *The Prize: The Epic Quest for Oil, Money and Power*. New York: Simon and Schuster, 1991.

ABOUT THE BOOK
AND EDITORS

As recent conflicts in Panama and the Persian Gulf demonstrate, we know much more about making war than we do about making peace. Such conflicts are not likely to disappear, and this volume reviews what has and hasn't worked in negotiating an end to war. Six case studies—ranging from World War I to the Persian Gulf crisis—illustrate a variety of actors, stakes, and strategies involved in the peacemaking process. Key turning points toward peace or deadlock are identified along the way. *Making Peace* also provides discussion questions, historical backgrounds, and theoretical introductions to show different—and differentially successful—avenues to peace.

Allan E. Goodman is associate dean of the School of Foreign Service at Georgetown University, director of the Master of Science in Foreign Service Program, professor of International Affairs, and coeditor of the recently released volume *The Central Intelligence Agency: An Instrument of Government to 1950.* **Sandra Clemens Bogart** is a project researcher in the Master of Science in Foreign Service Program at Georgetown University.